# The Fledglings
## The Story of HMS Fledgling

Graham Bebbington

with

Foreword by Professor Christine King
Vice-Chancellor & Chief Executive,
Staffordshire University

and

Preface by Commodore Annette Picton RN
Chief Naval Officer for Women

# Acknowledgments

I am especially grateful to Professor Christine King and Commodore Annette Picton for writing the foreword and preface respectively.

In addition to those quoted in the text or source notes, I acknowledge most gratefully the assistance of the following:
C. S. (Bill) Drake, Richard A. Durrant, Charles V. Rolfe, Bill Cowan, Ken West,
Mrs Phyllis Beveridge, Ray C. Sturtivant, Mrs Margaret Moorcroft, Mrs Muriel Dyson, Shaun Farrelly for providing information on the locally based American forces during World War II and for permission to reproduce illustrations from The Yarnfield Yankee, and M. C. Smelik, Maria Helson & Gerard Mutsaars for assistance with translation.

Gratitude is also expressed to:
Mrs. D. M. A. Randall, Head of Archive Services, Staffordshire County Council.
The librarians and staff of Eccleshall, Holmcroft and Newcastle-under-Lyme libraries.
The Secretary, The Association of Royal Navy Officers.
The Editors of Navy News, The Wren, and the Sentinel.
The staff of the Fleet Air Arm Museum, Yeovilton.
The Royal Naval Museum, Portsmouth.
The Imperial War Museum, in particular Peter Simkins.

My friend Dr Joan Delin kindly read through my final draft and made a number of extremely valuable suggestions which I was happy to incorporate. I am deeply indebted to her.

Finally, my wife Lynne Margaret has, as usual, shared in all the pleasures and pain of research and assisted with everything from typing to proof reading.

Every endeavour has been made to trace source material. If, inadvertently, any copyright has been infringed, the author offers his apology and will correct any omission in any subsequent edition.

**CHURNET VALLEY BOOKS**
1 King Street, Leek, Staffordshire. ST13 5NW 01538 399033
thebookshopleek.co.uk
© Graham Bebbington and Churnet Valley Books 2003
ISBN 1 897949 97 9

# CONTENTS

Foreword by Professor Christine E. King DL

Preface by Commodore Annette M. Picton RN

Introduction

Bibliography

Cover photographs courtesy of Dorothy Oates and Helen Proctor

# Dedicated to all who served at HMS Fledgling, Mill Meece

*'Almighty God, who makest the clouds thy chariot and who walkest upon the wings of the wind, we commend to thy Fatherly protection all who ride the skies in the service of the Fleet, and those in whose work they trust'*

Fleet Air Arm prayer

Wren air mechanics on the airfield of HMS Fledgling.
*Courtesy of Dorothy Oates*

# FOREWORD

The history of the Second World War continues to be written. The more we research and reflect on this important aspect of the past, the more we come to understand the present.

Like all good local history, this story has its own fascination. As we dip into the lives of the people stationed at HMS Fledgling in North Staffordshire, we learn of their training, their work, and their outings around the locality. We observe something of the impact they, in turn, had on a part of the country which had been fairly isolated from outside influences. We see women with freedom and a variety of roles, just before the 1950s placed them firmly back in the home.

The War changed the way we lived and worked and thought. Nothing was ever quite the same again. Whether we remember these times or not, this history of one small part of that experience has a lot to teach us. It also provides a really good read!

Professor Christine E. King DL
Vice-Chancellor & Chief Executive,
Staffordshire University

A wartime view of women at work by Dame Laura Knight.

## PREFACE

I was delighted to be asked to write the preface to this book.

Members of the Women's Royal Naval Service became liable for sea service on 1st September 1990, and the WRNS was integrated into the Royal Navy on 1st November 1993. Graham Bebbington's book on the history of HMS Fledgling at Mill Meece serves as a timely reminder that women who joined the services during the Second World War were very much the trailblazers for women who choose a career in today's Armed Forces.

Mill Meece in North Staffordshire was the location of the first purely WRNS technical training establishment for air mechanics and was set up in 1943. The author has combined a detailed history of the local area with personal insights from 'the Fledglings' who passed through the portals at Mill Meece. The result is a fascinating and engrossing book which ensures that HMS Fledgling's vital role has its own niche in the history of women in the services.

Annette Picton
Commodore RN
Chief Naval Officer
for Women

Women at war - ATS, WRNS, WAAF, Ambulance Corps, Land Army

# INTRODUCTION

Travelling along the A519 between Eccleshall and Newcastle-under-Lyme, it is difficult to imagine how this attractive and tranquil area of Staffordshire was dramatically changed during World War II.

Not only was the infamous Royal Ordnance Factory (Factory 55) hurriedly carved out of the countryside at nearby Swynnerton, but the area also became the home to thousands of munition workers and U.S. troops.

Also in the environs were hundreds of Wrens, based at HMS Fledgling in Mill Meece. Yet for all its importance, and the establishment having a number of claims to fame, HMS Fledgling is largely forgotten. Principally, it was the first purely WRNS technical training establishment. Furthermore, it was then the only naval air station fully manned by the Royal Navy, although there were one or two instructors who had transferred from the RAF to the Fleet Air Arm. In addition, as the war progressed, HMS Fledgling went on to fulfil another important role, that of training Dutch and Canadian ground crew personnel. Although not unusual in today's armed forces, HMS Fledgling is also believed to have been the first to possess a mixed officers' mess.

This then, is an attempt to rediscover the story of HMS Fledgling. To my knowledge, no previous attempt has been made to record this unique and important period in North Staffordshire's history.

Graham Bebbington

Also by Graham Bebbington

The Loggerheads Project (Newcastle Borough Council)

Pit Boy to Prime Minister (University of Keele)

A Brief Life (Isle of Wight County Press)

Trentham At War (Churnet Valley)

Ship Without Water (Churnet Valley)

# CHAPTER 1

# WOMEN AT WAR

*'... without allowing the women of Britain to enter the struggle as they desire to, we should fail utterly to bear our fair share of the burden which France and Britain have jointly assumed.'*

Winston S. Churchill 27th January 1940

Without the contribution of women during World War II it is likely that Britain would not have been victorious. Whilst not killing the enemy soldiers directly, nor storming enemy machine gun posts, they nevertheless risked their lives daily to maintain vital ammunition supplies for the armed forces, and also helped to keep the Country fed. These are merely two examples of the many tasks undertaken on the home front by female labour.

Working conditions in the munitions factories were extremely unhealthy and dangerous, and many women suffered serious injury and loss of limbs. Likewise, a number employed in the agriculture workforce, helping to provide food, were injured by farm machinery. At this time women generally were, in a way, experiencing a form of liberation, a situation they would not have encountered in peace time. According to tradition, they had been raised and educated to produce children and, suddenly, they were made aware, and took advantage, of other opportunities. However, enemy bombs do not discriminate, and as a result of their particular work or exposure to danger, many lost their lives or were severely injured. Yet my impression is that there appears to be little recognition of this, nor of women's contribution to the war effort generally, although at the time of writing certain politicians are attempting to remedy the situation.

It is not unusual to see advertisements in today's newspapers, or on television, proclaiming that it can be a woman's life in the modern armed services. Yet we seem to have forgotten that there were 640,000 in uniform during World War II. By 1943, more than 56,000 'ack ack' girls had joined the Royal Artillery Anti-Aircraft Command alone! Others were employed elsewhere in such 'acceptable' tasks as nursing and clerical work, but a number were also engaged on more 'specialist' duties such as delivering aircraft to Fighter Command, or driving 3 ton vehicles containing heavy cargo consisting of everything from stores to powerful explosives. In addition, there were those who delivered vital despatches through the black-out using high powered motor cycles.

There were 126 officers and 1,475 ratings in the WRNS in September 1939. The evacuation of Dunkirk then decided the destiny of almost every able bodied person in Britain. All three branches of the armed forces urgently needed more women in order to release men to fight. As a consequence, by the end of 1940, the

WRNS establishment had increased to 561 officers and 9,439 ratings. Many of the latter saw service as cooks in the early part of the War, and during the Dunkirk period they helped provide vital meals in improvised canteens for the men who had returned from the beaches, having had little or nothing to eat for days prior to evacuation. At the outbreak of war, there were 384 cooks, but by the end of 1940 this figure had increased to 1,082. Also in that year, the first courses for WRNS ratings began at a Royal Navy Cookery School.

Telephone switchboard training for WRNS ratings also began in 1940. This was followed with courses for teleprinter operators, mail clerks, visual signallers, wireless operators, meteorologists and drivers.

A number of Wrens were also engaged on the ULTRA team deciphering the captured German Enigma computer like code machine at Bletchley Park, whilst others manned boats, or repaired and fired guns.

The variety of jobs in which they were employed appears endless. With Fleet Air Arm maintenance now an option, courses for this particular category of Wren rating were organised alongside those of their male counterparts at such establishments as HMS Daedalus II, the RNATE at Clayton Hall, near Newcastle-under-Lyme. However, in view of the demand, the <u>first</u> purely WRNS technical training establishment for air mechanics was opened at Mill Meece in 1943.

Whilst the location of HMS Fledgling seemed in some ways idyllic, being situated in the beautiful undulating North Staffordshire countryside, there was one great disadvantage. The establishment was situated immediately to the rear of the Royal Ordnance Factory, Swynnerton - not the most ideal of situations! Consequently, many of the Wrens who trained there have adverse memories of the factory, and thus have mixed feelings about their period of service in North Staffordshire.

Women of the former Civil Air Guard became a section of the Air Transport Auxiliary Service in 1940.

# CHAPTER 2

# FACTORY 55

*'... a place of strange lights and explosions of sorts, and steam rising from various points - very spooky in the dark.'*

Former PO Wren Air Fitter (E) Jean Williams (nee Webb)[1]

At the beginning of World War II, 24 Royal Ordnance Factories were built in various parts of Britain to meet the urgent need for armaments and munitions. In Staffordshire, a site near the peaceful, tightly knit community of Swynnerton was chosen. Some 800 acres of rich and attractive countryside was requisitioned, principally from the Swynnerton and Cotes estates, much to the indignation of farmers and local residents. Although having a modest beginning, the factory eventually became the largest munitions producing plant in Europe, with perimeter security fencing alone measuring 15 miles in length.

ROF 55 Swynnerton was a *'filling factory'* and it played an extremely important role in Britain's war effort. Shell, bomb and land mine cases, together with fuses and high explosives such as TNT, were transported there for assembly into the finished product. Not surprisingly, it was a site much sought after by the Luftwaffe on its nightly bombing raids. In any event, during the blitz period, North Staffordshire seemed to be on the main route for enemy bombers attacking other big cities, particularly Liverpool and Manchester. However, there are those to this day who strongly contend that the factory escaped annihilation as a result of the frequent mists which shroud the Meece Valley thus hiding it from the eyes of enemy air crews. Having said that, a number recall the traitor William Joyce boasting on radio of a successful raid on Swynnerton. Joyce, of course, was the notorious 'Lord Haw-Haw' whose propaganda broadcasts from Germany were designed to sap the resolve of the British during the dark years of World War II.

Prior to the War, Swynnerton was a sleepy, old world village, a pleasant quiet backwater, with most of its population of 900 employed in agriculture. This changed dramatically with the building of the Royal Ordance Factory which at its peak employed between 25,000 and 30,000 personnel working on a three shift system. The predominance of the nearby pottery industry meant that there was already a tradition of working women, and a readily identifiable source of female labour. Nevertheless, this was to prove insufficient, and eventually thousands of young women either volunteered, or were drafted from all parts of the Country.

Some of the girls were only 18 years old and very immature, according to Mrs Cynthia Morley who was a local WPC at the time. Not having left home before, they found working at the munitions factory extremely difficult, not to mention also adjusting to the shift pattern. A few attempted to run away, but were caught and treated as 'deserters'. Offenders were subsequently brought before the Courts and jailed for a short period, merely *'to put the fear of God into them'* recalls Cynthia.

Having dealt with a number of such cases, she was involved with escort and similar duties whilst at the same time *'feeling sorry for those concerned.'* [2]

Thousands commuted in daily, whilst others stayed at specially built residential hostels named after famous naval heroes and mariners - Beatty, Drake, Duncan, Frobisher, Howard, Nelson and Raleigh. The resultant amount of increased traffic in the area was soon to have a *'serious effect'* on farmers and local residents. After receiving a number of complaints, Stone Rural District Council drew the attention of the Police and the Minister of Transport to the matter with a view to *'regulating the traffic'* in a bid to ease the situation.[3]

There were also complaints about the deterioration of the bus services to Stafford due to the coaches being required for *'transportation of war workers'* in the area.[4] Those travelling in by rail averaged 8,000 daily. To accommodate this increase, the 1.5 mile Cold Meece branch line was constructed in 1941 to serve the ROF. One of the busiest stations in the Midlands, it

The Mill Meece, Swynnerton, Yarnfield area, and the various wartime establishments.

nevertheless was a 'ghost line', shrouded in wartime secrecy, never appearing in any public railway timetable.[5]

The factory bore little resemblance to a conventional one, consisting of some

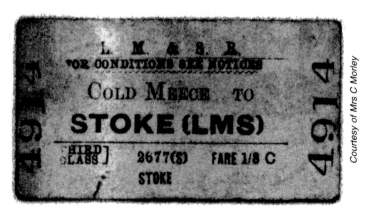

*Courtesy of Mrs C Morley*

2,000 or so small buildings. These were separated from each other by substantial distances, and often by large earth mounds and walls to reduce the high risk of explosions. Even so, of all the munition establishments, those engaged in filling processes, such as the Swynnerton plant, were the most dangerous. This involved handling extremely high explosives, thus carrying a possibility of serious injury or even death for employees. In addition, there was a high risk to health from the toxicity of many of the materials used.

Under its Superintendent, Mr A. Dawes Robinson, security at ROF Swynnerton was naturally tight. The dangers faced daily by employees were evident in the precautions that they had to endure. Mrs Wyn Coleby (nee Mann) recalls that, on arrival, a special pass had to be shown to the Police. Then, on entering the gates *'the contribution box'* was situated where cigarettes, matches, snuff etc had to be deposited. After undergoing a security check at 'the shift house' Mrs Coleby also recollects being *'searched for that stray cigarette or matches etc'* before changing into special clothing and rubber boots. In addition, all metal objects were banned with the exception of wedding rings, which had to be covered. Also banned was the wearing of jewellery or hairgrips.

Such careful procedures certainly brought home to Wyn and her colleagues, the constant risks being run in the handling of explosive materials.[6] Nevertheless, as the late Councillor May Blakemore recalled - *'explosions happened from time to time, someone losing a limb or worse.'* Since having worked at Swynnerton, she claimed that *'her nerves had never been the same.'*[7]

To deal with emergency situations, the Ordnance Factory had its own well-equipped Fire Brigade which consisted of four stations, one staffed entirely by females. Such was the Brigade's reputation, that it was called to assist local fire fighters during the blitz on Coventry in 1940 when 1,400 bombs were dropped on the city in a heavy raid lasting more than 10 hours.[8]

Surprisingly, there appear to be no accurate figures of fatalities, injuries, or illness, resulting from munitions work. Having said that, barriers of secrecy still shield aspects of World War II even today. What is certain is that many who worked at Swynnerton during the war years were profoundly affected by their experience. Some lost limbs, or were left with severe physical disabilities, whilst others were psychologically scarred. It was also not unusual at the time to see in the Potteries area some of the ROF female operatives with yellow skin or hair. This resulted from handling a yellow powder used to fill landmines. It also made many of them ill.

Some records appertaining to ROF Swynnerton have survived and clearly illustrate the dangers to munition workers which were associated with their employment. For example, on 20th December 1943, an explosion occurred at the factory killing three male employees. A subsequent Board of Inquiry conducted by HM Chief Inspector of Explosives found that *'the three men were literally blown to pieces and their remains widely scattered.'* The major body parts of two of the deceased were reported as only being identifiable by the jerseys they were

The German raids on Coventry, 14th November 1940.

wearing. The third could only be identified by *'the remnants of his watch, chain and penknife.'* Some human remains were found as far away as 200 yards from the site of the explosion. [9]

But for all this, ROF Swynnerton had a remarkable working atmosphere and camaraderie. A wonderful spirit of friendship helped the workers face the dangers and hardships of their daily tasks. Employees organised an amazing social life including dances, film shows, pantomines and pageants. Also, being of a generous nature, they were prepared to share their entertainment and social life with others. Armed forces personnel serving in the vicinity, including those from HMS Fledging, were invited to the functions which were generally held in one or other of the halls of residence. If for no other reason, the Swynnerton employees are fondly remembered and held in high regard for this.

*Courtesy of the Artistic Director, The New Vic Theatre*

The play *I Don't Want to Set the World on Fire*, a lively and popular musical about the Swynnerton munition workers, performed at the New Victoria Theatre, Newcastle under Lyme.

*Courtesy of Dorothy Abcki and The New Vic Theatre*

Women munition workers at Swynnerton.

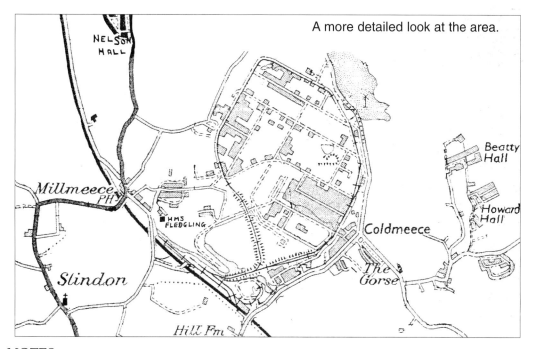

A more detailed look at the area.

## NOTES

1 Jean Williams. Letter to author 30 June 1997
2 Cynthia Morley. Telephone interview with author 28 March 2000
3 Minutes of Stone Rural District Council 21 December 1939 & 18 January 1940
4 Ibid 3 June 1943
5 Rex Christiansen & E.W. Miller *The North Staffordshire Railway* (David & Charles, 1971)
6 Wyn Coleby. Letter to author 9 October 1997
7 May Blakemore. *Reminiscences* in *Further accounts of Silverdale life* (OEC Publications, Stoke-on-Trent 1999) p15
8 John H.Emery. Interview with author 2nd November 2001 Also Mrs M. Collinson. Telephone interview 21 November 2001
9 Public Record Office. Accident Report No.F228. Ref SUPP 5/1212

Visit of Mrs Eleanor Roosevelt, wife of US President, to ROF Swynnerton. Nov 1942.

Visit of King George VI and Queen Elizabeth to ROF Swynnerton. Feb 1942.

Employees of ROF Swynnerton enjoying a pageant at Raleigh Hall, Summer 1942.

*Courtesy of John H. Emery.*

ROF Swynnerton Fire Brigade, 1943.
Chief Fire Officer Bernard Faupel is seen centre front row; Assistant CFO Harold Emery, on his right.

# CHAPTER 3

# THE COMING OF HMS FLEDGLING

*'I'm told one can see the Wrekin on a clear day. It is farming country, gently undulating, with a lot of trees, little streams and dozens of intersecting lanes which are very pleasant for cycling.'*

Extract from diary of former 2/O Wren Mrs A.D. Deacon[1]

HMS Fledgling came into existence during an exciting period of World War II as the 8th Army launched a new offensive in Tunisia. The local *Staffordshire Advertiser* proclaimed *'Montgomery Strikes Again!'* and a German reporter was quoted as describing a British artillery night barrage as *'like a continuous thunderstorm!'* Huge gains were also reported in aerial combat with RAF and US fighters destroying 74 enemy aircraft (including 51 huge transporters) in *'the largest and most successful single engagement ever fought in African skies.'*[2]

Montgomery triumphant in North Africa 1943

Commissioned on 15th April 1943, the new training establishment was placed under the command of Captain Percy Ralph Passawer Percival. Promoted to Midshipman in 1903, Percival had risen steadily through the ranks to achieve a distinguished naval career. He had seen plenty of action during World War I and had been awarded the DSO following a skirmish with German destroyers off the Belgian coast on 21st March 1918. After the War, he continued in command of destroyers, eventually retiring from the service in 1932. Like many of his contemporaries, however, he was recalled to the colours in 1939 at the outbreak of World War II.[3] Percival and his popular Old English Sheepdog were familiar sights at the establishment and in the locality, and a few local residents

remember them fondly to this day. Described as *'a very pleasant person'*, he remained in charge of HMS Fledgling until its closure at the end of the War.[4]

HMS Fledgling has a number of claims to fame. Principally, it was the <u>first</u> purely WRNS technical training establishment, and also the first Naval Air Station fully manned by the Royal Navy, although there were one or two instructors who had transferred from the RAF to the Naval Air Branch (ie Fleet Air Arm).[5] The intention was to train Wren Air Mechanics, the introduction of which would eventually result in a saving of 25-30% of manpower for the Navy.[6] The instructors were a mixture of Navy and Air Branch Engineers. Lt.Commander W.E. Budge was in charge of training, and the only RN Officer with wings was the Air Gunnery Officer - Lt (A) P.C.S. Bagley who had the distinction of having held the King's Commission in the Army, RAF and the Navy. In all, there were approximately 40 instructors, mainly Chief Petty Officers or Petty Officers and some 20 naval ratings.

Records also show that the initial ship's company included Rev. P.B. Clear MA (Chaplain), Lt. Commander J.C.L. Willett RNVR (Paymaster), Surg. Lt M.C. Jenkins MRCS, LRCP, and two dentists - Surg. Lt (D) W.L. Oakes LDS and Miss H.H. Brett LDS. Although an air station for training Wren Air Mechanics, a contemporary magazine feature described the atmosphere of the establishment as being 'more nautical than aeronautical'.[7]

New arrivals at HMS Fledgling in 1943.
Betty Finn, who supplied the photo, is second left.

Fledgling's initial accommodation was in buildings taken over from the Ministry of Supply. Known locally as 'the Craftsmen's Houses', these had been hastily erected to accommodate the personnel engaged in constructing the Swynnerton munitions factory, after which they were surplus to requirements.[8] According to a contemporary report, much was accomplished in a short time by the ship's company to achieve satisfactory adaptation of the buildings to Admiralty requirements. Much of this was undertaken by maintenance staff from Fledgling's nearby 'parent' establishment - HMS Daedalus II - under Shipwright Lt S.C. McClounnan. PO Joiner Frank Plant can recall working at Fledgling where the Wrens *'spoiled him at times'*. He also admits to *'having to lock his door at night!'*

Having *'caught a packet'* from a German Stuka during the seige of Tobruk, Frank spent time recuperating from his injuries before being posted to North Staffordshire. He admitted, thankfully, that it was *'much quieter'* at Mill Meece than Tobruk.[9] A magazine feature written a few months after commissioning indicates that the buildings had *'adapted very well to the Admiralty scheme'*, and that the Officers' and Wrens' quarters were *'comfortable'*. Most of the workshops were said to be of *'a good size'* and if one or two of the classrooms seemed *'on the small size, they were adequate'*.[10]

Subsequently, the base also had additional accommodation in High Street, Eccleshall where a number of WRNS officers resided in a hostel.[11] Furthermore, as the ship's company consisted of a number of male and female officers, it was decided to create a mixed Officers' Mess. Its first elected President was Chief Wren Hilda Buckmaster, an early example of equality between the sexes.[12] Coming from

Courtesy of Dorothy Oates

Stafford Street, Eccleshall in the 1940s. The town was popular with the Wrens.

an old naval family, Miss Buckmaster had served as a Wren during World War I. A commanding and inspiring figure, she went on to have a distinguished career in the service.

One of the initial priorities of the first arrivals at HMS Fledgling was to clean, or *'spit and polish'* the accommodation and to assemble bunk beds etc., duties which former Wren Mary Kennedy was to experience. Having arrived at Stafford railway station, she and her colleagues were transported by naval transport to Mill Meece. This, in itself, was like *'a cloak and dagger exercise'* explained Mary, as the Petty Officer in charge was carrying sealed orders! They were not informed of their destination, but on arrival at Stafford, Mary recognised the town from earlier visits. Climbing into the vehicle at the station she and her colleagues set off into the countryside, eventually stopping at some *'very forbidding and heavily guarded gates'*. Scrutiny of a pass and papers followed, and the vehicle and its passengers were eventually allowed to enter the premises, after which the gates were immediately shut. It was only later that they learned that they had driven through the middle of ROF Swynnerton before reaching their new accommodation at what was to become HMS Fledgling! She explained that, at that time, there was no seperate access to the naval establishment. This was subsequently formed off Old Hall Lane where a guardroom was also erected. However, having a rare insight into the munitions factory is an experience that Mary has not forgotten!

Courtesy of Betty Finn

Wrens at HMS Fledgling, Mill Meece, relaxing off duty.

On arrival, the buildings and grounds allocated for the new training establishment were deserted and over the following fortnight or so, Mary and her party of colleagues strove to prepare the accommodation for the new arrivals. They were fortunate on having a superb PO Cook who fed them *'nobly'*, sustinence which was much appreciated after the hard work in preparing the camp. Shortly afterwards, a Second Officer Wren arrived to take charge temporarily, followed by a whole series of other personnel, including instructors. However, *'it was a great day'*. Mary recalls, *'when the higher ranking officers arrived, followed by the aircraft, and then the naval station suitably christened HMS Fledgling was ready to receive its first trainees'*.[13]

Amongst these was former Wren Betty Finn who thought that the accommodation at Mill Meece was *'luxurious'* after her previous posting at Balloch in Scotland. This, she recalled, consisted of *'old Nissen huts and mud everywhere'*! Betty described Fledgling's layout as *'terraced and mainly consisting of long brick single storey buildings. Each room contained two double bunks, chests of drawers and hanging space'*.[14] Former Wren Muriel Dyson (nee Greendale) was also among those first trainees to arrive at HMS Fledgling. She considered the camp to be *'well built, with all the modern conveniences, even in those far off days'*. It was also her first experience of central heating![15]

Thus, having assembled the ship's company, and greeted the first Wren trainee Air Mechanics, HMS Fledgling was ready for business.

NOTES

1    Imperial War Museum(IWM) Ref  89/17/1. p172
2    Staffordshire Advertiser  24 April 1943
3    Navy lists (various)
4    Diary of Mrs A.D.Deacon. IWM Ref 89/17/1. p171
5    This resulted from an earlier Government decision to transfer control of the FAA from the Air Ministry to the Admiralty. Prior to this, RAF personnel had been embarked on carriers and maintenance of flights had been their responsibility. See Winston S. Churchill *The Second World War Vol I. The Gathering Storm* (Penguin 1985) p 143
6    The Aeroplane  6 August 1943
7    Ibid
8    Mr J. Bennison Snr. Interview with author 3 March 1997
9    Frank Plant. Letter to author 20 April 1998
10   The Aeroplane op.cit
11   Stone Rural District Council - minutes of Eccleshall & Chebsey Sewerage & Water Supply Committee 9 August 1943
12   May Calvert. Letter quoted in The Wren February 1999
13   Mary Kennedy. Letters to author 17 August & 1 September 1997
14   Betty Finn. Letters to author (undated) February &  April 1997
15   Muriel Dyson. Letter to author 3 June 1997

Courtesy of Dorothy Oates

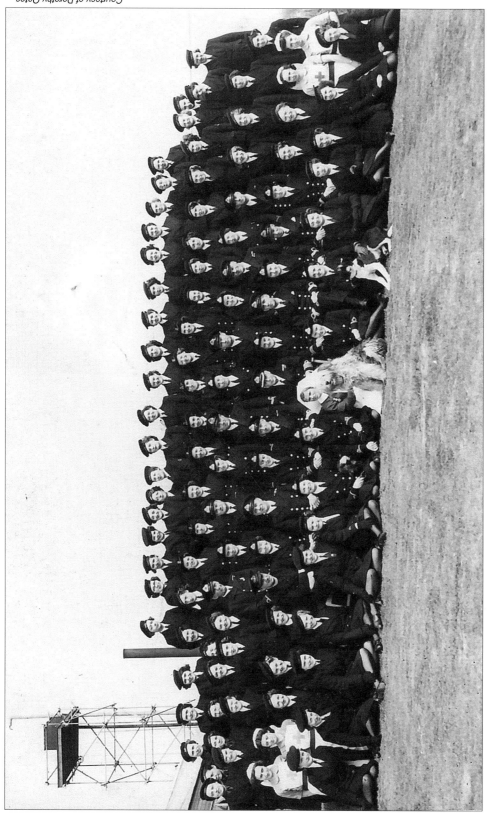

HMS Fledgling Ship's Company, 1943.

*Courtesy of Dorothy Oates*

View from the crossroads, Eccleshall.  The Town's public houses and cafes were popular venues.

*Courtesy of May Calvert*

Officers' Mess, HMS Fledgling, July 1943 - believed to be the first mixed mess.

" This is H.M.S. 'FLEDGLING' one of our establishments."

" Wrens, one teeny, weeny pace forward—march !"

# CHAPTER 4

# ABOARD SHIP

*'I was initially horrified when I heard I was going to the 'Black Country' - Arnold Bennett etc but thought that the area of Staffordshire was lovely.'*

Former Wren Pam Lawler (nee Hickman)[1]

Whilst conscription of single women between the ages of 20-30 years (the National Service Act (No.2)) had been announced in the press in late 1941, large numbers of them had already left 'boring' jobs and volunteered for the services or war work. Those who had joined the WRNS did so for a variety of reasons, some volunteering despite being in reserved occupations in civilian life. Others simply preferred to join the service rather than be directed to work in a munitions factory.

Many, like Jean Williams, volunteered because *'there was a war on - we all felt we wanted to do our bit!'* She had *'heard of the Wrens and liked the uniform'* and freely admitted that this was another reason for volunteering for the service.[2]

Indeed, all those Wren Trainee Air Mechanics who joined HMS Fledgling were volunteers. Nevertheless, they had been selected, to a point, the general standard of education being the School Certificate. Perhaps the most surprising aspect was their apparent lack of any previous association with, or even a

A uniform hemline for the Wrens: *'But supposing we all wore our skirts above the . . . er . . . 'Plimsoll Line,' as it were.'*

particular interest in aeronautics. Few had flown, and although they came from various backgrounds - actress, musician, dress designer, nurse, shop assistant etc - the majority were in clerical work. By contrast, the new recruits also included girls straight from boarding school, and young women who were already widows. Asked why they chose to be Air Mechanics, most thought that it would be interesting, whilst several thought that the electrical category especially would be useful when hostilities ceased. Others commented that they wished to work with their hands, but only a few expressed an actual desire to work in aeronautics.[3]

Generally, the girls tended to arrive at Mill Meece a day or so early to enable them to settle in before actually commencing their particular course. Coming to the establishment via various routes, a number had in fact already been working as Aircraft Checkers, a job previously undertaken by RAF personnel on loan to the Royal Navy. In the early days, some Wrens had received no basic training at all on arrival, whereas others had completed their first two weeks or so at such places as Mill Hill or Balloch. Former Wren Mary Kennedy recalled her training at Mill Hill where she was introduced to the delights of the inevitable *'square bashing'* by male regular instructors, some of whom made it clear that they did not approve of women *'in the service!'* Training at Mill Hill and other WRNS training depots also tended to include lectures on the Royal Navy and its chain of command, naval terms and general fatigues or domestic work. After successful completion of a written examination at the end of the basic training period, they were formally enrolled as Wrens.[4]

Those trainees joining HMS Fledgling had to come to terms quickly with the fact that, like all other Royal Navy shore establishments, it was considered to be a ship. Ground beyond its boundaries was, therefore, considered to be the sea! Personnel leaving the ship would line up for inspection at the guardroom before *'going ashore'* and this was termed *'the liberty boat'*. Those returning late were likely to be disciplined, the reason being that a real ship could have been under orders to sail. All newcomers were expected to become conversant with this traditional naval terminology. Everything centred on naval terms - the deck (ground), deckhead (ceiling), bulkheads (walls), companionways (passage & stairs), the heads (toilets), stand easy (tea break), and galley (kitchen) to name a few examples.

Jean Williams should have reported to Balloch for training but as a result of an outbreak of dysentery there, she was drafted straight to Mill Meece. Describing her arrival at Standon Bridge Halt, Jean wrote to her parents at the time that she had been *'whisked off to HMS Fledgling with a number of 'real Wrens' in naval transport.'* Having arrived late in the evening, she was provided with supper before reporting to the linen room where everything had to be signed for - *'three lovely fleecy blankets, one pillow, one mattress cover, one pillow slip, one pair sheets, and a patterned stiff blue coverlet with crown, anchor, and wreath patterned in the centre'*. Initially, Jean found the establishment to be *'the most awful maze - up steps and down steps'* and she was *'always getting lost among the huts!'* Nonetheless, she found herself in good amiable company and soon settled in.

Jean was to write home regularly during her period at Mill Meece, giving details of life on board HMS Fledgling and even enclosing sketch plans of the establishment and locality. However, unlike the experience of many service personnel at the time, Jean's correspondence was not censored! She admits now, that the diagrams do appear like 'careless talk' and agrees some of the detail could have been most useful had it fallen into the wrong hands. Thankfully, the correspondence has survived!

Before actually commencing her Air Mechanic (E) course, Jean spent a three week probationary period at HMS Fledgling, and in one letter she gave details of a typical day at the establishment -

| | |
|---|---|
| 07.45 | Breakfast |
| 08.25 | Muster on quarterdeck - Divisions with Chaplain |
| 08.45 | Squad drill |
| 09.15 | Working party |
| 10.15. | Stand easy |
| 10.30 | Working party |
| 11.15 | Lecture on Standing Orders |
| 12.00 | Lunch |
| 14.00 | Muster on quarterdeck for PT or games |
| 15.15 | Stand easy |
| 15.30 | Security lecture |
| 16.15 | First aid lecture |
| 18.00 | Secure (off duty) |
| 18.15 | Supper |
| 21.30 | In cabins |
| 22.00 | Pipe down [5] |

Another early arrival, former Leading Wren Amy Mansfield (nee Herbert), a member of the ship's company, was one of a number to comment about the problem of smoke from neighbouring ROF Swynnerton. Apparently, it was a regular occurence that as the parade was assembling on Fledgling's quarterdeck, testing of ammunition would commence coincidentally at the munitions factory, resulting in the parade ground and crew *'covered in a haze or fog!'*[6] Smoke from ROF Swynnerton was a constant source of complaint and came to the attention of officials of Stone Rural District Council. As a result, a number of meetings were held with the factory's management, including Mr Blanch, the Assistant Superintendent, in an attempt to alleviate the problem. Times being what they were, no detail is given of the discussions which took place, but the complaints to the Council are recorded.[7]

Napoleon is reputed to have observed that *'an army marches on its stomach.'* Whether a similar quotation exists in respect of the navy I am uncertain, but it is a fact that its personnel cannot perform their responsibilities without the necessary sustenance. This was obviously appreciated by the Admiralty and at HMS Fledgling, despite rationing and the war situation, the food had an excellent reputation. The following are examples of meals from one day's fare:

| | |
|---|---|
| Breakfast | cereal; sausage, bacon & fried bread; toast & marmlade |
| Lunch | chop,carrots & potatoes; rice & raisin pudding [8] |

Tea and some form of refreshments were also available at break times (stand easy). Fledgling personnel were also fortunate being situated in a country area. Fresh produce and milk for the galley could easily be obtained from local farms etc. Members of the crew were also able to supplement their food intake with fresh fruit from shops in the nearby small market town of Eccleshall, or neighbouring farms. Jean Williams explained that only receiving 11 shillings per fortnight in pay, she and her colleagues were unable to go on shopping sprees, but found the shopkeepers in Eccleshall *'very nice and obliging'*. Service personnel found the town, formerly the seat of the Bishops of Lichfield, a most pleasant place with its historic inns and attractive wide High Street, and *'a run ashore'* there was a welcome break. There was also a popular WVS canteen there where cups of coffee or tea could be purchased, together with sandwiches and cake - all good value, being *'very cheap!'* [9]

In the meantime, there was encouraging news on the war front. Having skilfully planned and boldly executed the invasion of Sicily, the allies then invaded Italy, and fought with such success

Supply Branch, HMS Fledgling. Dorothy Oates who supplied the photo is in the foreground with 'Corky'

that before long, war-weary Italian troops offered unconditional surrender. At this point , too, the media began to report on the German aircraft  industry's inability to expand sufficiently to satisfy the requirements of their front line squadrons. Factories were having to work at full pressure to meet  the demands caused by defeats at Stalingrad and in North Africa. In those two campaigns alone, the Luftwaffe had lost practically an entire year's production.[10]

NOTES

1     Pam Lawler. Letter to author 11 June 1997
2     Jean Williams. Letter to author 30 June 1997
3     The Aeroplane op.cit
4     Mary Kennedy. Various correspondence to author
5     Jean Williams, unpublished correspondence to her parents dated September 1943
6     Amy Mansfield. Letter to author 23 September 1998
7     Minutes of Stone Rural District Council 17 June & 30 December 1943
8     Jean Williams op.cit
9     Jean Williams. Letter to author 26 July 1997
10    The Aeroplane op.cit

Wrens of the Ship's company, HMS Fledgling. Officers, Petty Officers, Cooks and Stewards. Wren Amy Herbert (now Mansfield) who supplied the photo, is on the left in the foreground.

Officers of the Ship's Company, HMS Fledgling, with the Commanding Officer, Captain P.R.P. Percival DSO in the centre.

*Courtesy of May Calvert*

HMS Fledgling, Morning Divisions on the quarterdeck, 1943.

Ref. Dr/7M.

WOMEN'S ROYAL NAVAL SERVICE,
Queen Anne's Mansions,
London, S.W.1.

14ᵗʰ Sept. 1943 .

Dear Madam,

With reference to your application for enrolment in the Women's Royal Naval Service, you are hereby instructed to report for training as a Probationary Wren on ____ to the Officer-in-Charge, W.R.N.S., Training & Drafting Depot, Ridgeway, Mill Hill, London, N.W.7.

On arrival in London the quickest route is by underground direct to Mill Hill East Station. A W.R.N.S. Regulating Petty Officer wearing a white band on her arm with the letters R.P.O. on it will be on duty at this station and you should report to her for detailed instructions regarding the short distance to Ridgeway.

You should reach the Training Depot NOT LATER THAN 3 P.M. Those living in or near London must report before 12 noon. In the event of your travelling a long distance, and being unable to arrive by that time, please note that after 7 p.m. you should take a Barnet train, changing at Finchley Central where the Mill Hill East trains wait at an adjacent platform. Single deck buses No. 240 meet every train at the above (Mill Hill East) and stop outside the Depot.

All luggage is to be left at Mill Hill East Station and will be collected by the Depot van at regular intervals.

Enclosed is a railway warrant which should be exchanged for a ticket at your Booking Office. If in any difficulty with regard to transport when you reach London, telephone Whitehall 9444, extension 170.

You will probably be required to stay in the Depot for a fortnight, possibly longer, but you must be prepared after you have been enrolled to proceed direct from the Depot to the Port to which you will be drafted.

Also enclosed is a list of serviceable clothing for your guidance.

Kindly fill in and return Section C below immediately.

Yours faithfully,

E. M. WILBERFORCE

for Director, W.R.N.S.                P.T.O.

DO NOT REPORT IF YOU ARE ILL. You cannot be accepted for training if you are suffering from feverish cold, influenza, abnormal temperature or other illness. In this case you should communicate with W.R.N.S. Headquarters, forwarding a doctor's certificate as to the probable length of deferment needed and return your travelling warrant. If you are able to telephone Whitehall 9444, extension 170, please do so.

## PROBATIONARY PERIOD.

### NATIONAL SERVICE CANDIDATES.

The privilege of withdrawing at will from the W.R.N.S. during the probationary period is not extended to recruits entered under the National Service Acts. Should such recruits prove unsuitable for the Service, however, they may be discharged forthwith during the first fourteen days at the discretion of the Director, W.R.N.S.

### VOLUNTEERS.

(1)　　　All recruits must, on entry, sign a Preliminary Form of Enrolment to cover the period of probation. On termination of probation they will, if acceptable and willing to continue to serve in the W.R.N.S., be required to complete a Form of Enrolment for the duration of the war.

(2)　　　The normal period of probation will be 14 days.

(3)　　　During the period of probation, either the probationer or the W.R.N.S. authorities may terminate the arrangement at will at any time, and the probationer is, in such circumstances, entitled to pay, etc., up to and including the day on which she leaves.

(4)　　　If, during the probationary period, sickness, injury or death, arises from causes not accepted as attributable to service in the W.R.N.S., probationary Wrens will not be entitled to claim for any pay or allowances during sick absence from duty nor to free medical treatment, nor to burial at the expense of the Crown. This does not debar a probationary Wren from such medical treatment as may be necessary to make her fit to travel home, or, alternatively, to resume duty as a probationer if the sickness is expected to be of short duration.

(5)　　　If, during the period of probation, sickness, injury or death, arises from causes accepted as attributable to service in the W.R.N.S., the probationer will be entitled to be dealt with in all respects as an enrolled member of the W.R.N.S.

Some WRNS paperwork from 1943.

Dy/.3.    (Revised 15.3.42).

Women's Royal Naval Service.

Probationary Wrens, on reporting to the Training Depot, should bring with them the minimum amount of ordinary civilian clothing for a fortnight. The following requirements are desirable, but it must be clearly understood that it is not necessary to expend coupons or money in acquiring new articles of clothing:-

 1 overcoat or raincoat.
 1 hat or scarf for use in wet weather.
 2 nightdresses or pairs of pyjamas.
 1 or 2 pairs of walking shoes (low heels essential).
 1 pair of indoor shoes.
 The usual underclothing, stockings, etc. (marked please).
 Toilet requisites (including sufficient soap (and soap flakes if desired) or soap coupons, for fourteen days; also hair brush and tooth brush).
 2 pairs ankle socks.

The following articles MUST BE BROUGHT by every Probationary Wren:-

 Identity Card.
 Ration Cards
 Clothing Coupons.
 Respirator.
 Torch.
 Unemployment and National Health Insurance Cards.

Underclothing is not provided gratuitously when uniform is issued.    A grant of 45/- is made in lieu.    Articles can be purchased from Service sources after enrolment.

One blue overall is provided immediately on arrival.    This is in the form of a coat dress, and constitutes sufficient wear for indoors of a uniform nature.

Sports equipment including shorts, slacks, bathing suits and gym shoes SHOULD BE BROUGHT for use in Physical Training if applicants already have these in their possession.

As, during air-raids, it may be necessary to sleep in shelters, the following articles are also desirable:-

 1 rug or coloured blanket.
 1 dressing gown.

One suitcase only is permitted.    This should be sufficiently large to contain the civilian clothing which is brought to the Depot as well as uniform. No Probationary Wren should bring with her more clothes than are required for the probationary fortnight.

No food or drink should be brought or sent to the Training Depot.

131AdTRB.

# CHAPTER 5

# LEARNING THE ROPES

*'When I consider how concentrated the course was, I marvel to think we actually emerged capable to work an aircraft and keep it in the air'.*

Former Wren Betty (Mickey) Finn[1]

Training courses at HMS Fledgling provided for four categories of Air Mechanics - Airframe (A), Engine (E), Electrician (L), and Ordnance or armament (O). All courses lasted for approximately eighteen weeks, with trainees usually being granted a week's leave halfway through the programme. Examinations were held every four weeks or so with marks of 40% resulting in failure, and 50% a warning. Candidates failing in one exam were likely to be put back for two weeks to enable a further attempt to be made and, hopefully, a better result to be achieved. Only two failures were allowed, but results at Fledgling in August 1943 showed such cases to be extremely few. [2]

Initially, training was practically the same for each category, with lectures on the history of flying, types of aircraft used in the Fleet Air Arm, duties of a Naval Air Station, aerodrome procedures, flight routine and explanations of aeronautical terms. A visit to an aerodrome generally concluded this section. All trainees attended classes for extra and applied mathematics, and initially learned how to acquire skills in the use of tools for their particular trade. Training also emphasised that, unlike in the civilian workplace, there were no fixed hours. Maintenance personnel's duty was to get all aircraft serviced, or repaired, as soon as possible, to enable them to be airborne again. As one rating on the Malta convoy of 1942 observed: 'we just work on till the job's done!'[3]

In the establishment's formative period, Ordnance trainees received much of their training at HMS Daedalus II, a Royal Navy Artificer Training Establishment (RNATE) and Fledgling's 'parent' unit, at nearby Newcastle-under-Lyme. This was the system until its own facilities were available at Mill Meece. Based at Clayton Hall, Daedalus II had extensive training resources, the Admiralty having requisitioned a number of public buildings when the establishment was hurriedly evacuated to the town from Lympne in 1940. Whilst being dispersed in numerous buildings in different parts of the town, Daedalus II was nevertheless described at the time as 'a triumph of ingenious administration'.[4] The requisitioned properties also included the Parish Hall for use as an armoury and classroom. Here, equipment included a Bolton & Paul hydraulic gun turret for training purposes.

Trainee Ordnance Mechanics had the benefit of being able to learn about .303 and .505 Browning machine guns, 20mm cannon and every aircraft gun in service with the Fleet Air Arm, also being taught how to strip, clean and re-assemble them. In addition, they became familiar with different types of ammunition and recoil systems and learned just about everything that was likely to go wrong and how to correct faults or remedy repairs swiftly and efficiently. Practical work was also done in 'bomb alley' which contained models of all types of bombs in use on naval aircraft.

Pam Lawler recalls being transported daily into Newcastle, there being eighteen girls on her course 'O1'. She also particularly remembers a '*charming*' civilian instructor Mr Fitzpatrick. Pam found Newcastle-under-Lyme to be 'a pleasant market town', but considered the Potteries towns to be '*rather grim!*'[5] Another Ordnance Trainee, Eileen Smith (nee Keefe), remembers CPO Tim Gavin who was their instructor for brazing, soldering etc. As part of the course, the girls had to make a usable spanner from a rough piece of metal. In doing so, the girls quickly learned that by encouraging Tim to talk about his experiences and interesting '*sea stories*', he would virtually complete the product for them!

Eileen recalls that '*he really was a wonderful man, so patient with them that they all made sure that they passed his part of the course with good marks to ensure that the powers that be appreciated what a good instructor he was.*' Likening Fledgling to a boarding school, Eileen explained that they had to be back '*on board*' by 9.30pm weekdays, and 10.30pm on Saturdays. However, she felt that such restrictions were probably justified, given the amount of studying that they were required to do.[6]

Trainee Airframe Mechanics first learned how to use hand and power operated drills, practise riveting, simple heat treatment, tapping and filing etc. Having become acquainted with tools, they then progressed to splicing of cable and rope, fabric repairs on damaged fuselages, preliminary and advanced rigging, hydraulics and pneumatics, metal repairs, aircraft maintenance and flight routine. Towards the end of the course, these particular trainees also undertook between-

*Courtesy of Mrs Pam Lawler*

Wrens of Class 01, HMS Fledgling, under instruction of CPO Worsley
at the Armoury of HMS Daedalus, Newcastle-under-Lyme.

*Courtesy of May Calvert*

Airframe trainees repairing the wing float of a 'Walrus', HMS Fledgling. July 1943.

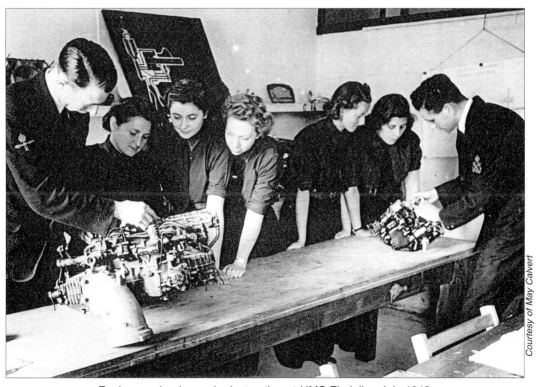

*Courtesy of May Calvert*

Engine mechanics under instruction at HMS Fledgling July 1943.

flight and daily inspections, changing wheels and laying out flare paths. Even today, Betty Finn marvels at *'how concentrated the course was, and that in a few months they had learned the intricacies of aerodynamics, metal work, hydraulics and pneumatics, and other skills.'*[7] Former L/Wren Q/S Jean Margaret Sole (nee Barr) retains memories in particular of the use of electric drills and in precision filing to a tolerance of one thousandth of an inch, with the many tests and examinations as the course progressed. She recalls using her metal work knowledge in repairing and putting patches over bullet holes inflicted on both the canvas of the Swordfish and on the metal aircraft which were frequently *'strafed'* on the open airfield by enemy bullets. Subsequently, she became qualified to sign the vital Form 700 which certified that a fighter aircraft or bomber was fit to fly.[8]

The initial phase of the Trainee Engine Mechanics' course was also spent on acquiring skills involving use of tools. In addition, they learned about various types of metals, different 'fastenings' (nuts, bolts, washers etc), drilling, and tapping etc. Subsequently, they progressed to the principles of the internal combustion engine, magnetos, carburettors, airscrews, advanced engines and aerodrome procedures. Engines used at the establishment included Merlin, Pegasus, Taurus, Gipsy I, Armstrong Siddeley Cheetah, Gipsy Queen, and a Pratt & Whitney Twin Wasp. Working in pairs, the trainees stripped the engines, removed the cylinders and re-assembled, also learning how to re-assemble airscrews, and fit spinners. Before completing the course, each trainee would have assisted in removing an engine from an aircraft and then reinstalled it. Former Wren Helen Proctor still retains her 'gen' book and looking through it today finds that she is 'amazed at the amount of information which was imparted to them.'[9] Jean Williams also recalls having *'a great time'* during the basic part of the course *'converting a small rectangular piece of rusty mild steel into a 'tombstone', suitably chiselled, hacksawed, filed, drilled and exactly shaped within two thou., and, of course, gleaming!'*[10]

Electrician trainees, like their colleagues in other trades, began by learning how to use their particular tools, also being taught about elementary soldering, simple circuits, ignition and harness circuits, and then progressing to electric airscrews, and bomb and torpedo release circuits. Other subjects included maintenance of landing lights and night flying equipment. An amount of practical work was carried out on boards of varying sizes fixed to walls. Small boards incorporated circuits for cockpits and/or navigation and landing lights, whereas a larger board taking up a whole wall contained complete circuits for every electrical instrument on an operational aircraft. Another display featured cockpit instruments linked to various types of bomb release gear. These trainees were expected to learn all circuits by heart, enabling them to detect and repair faults quickly. When qualified, they also were able to sign the vital Form 700 certifying that an aircraft was fit to fly. Former Wren Joan Garvey remembers the course as *'quite intensive, particularly as she knew nothing about electrical systems to begin with!'*[11]

Former Wren Margaret Tansey (nee Curry) also describes her five month electrical course at HMS Fledgling as 'intensive.' She recalls that when she first saw the interior of the cockpit of a Seafire, she was *petrified at the sight of the electrical controls and thought that she would never cope.'* Nonetheless, she did qualify as an Air Mechanic (L), working on a Barracuda, perhaps the most disliked aircraft of the war period. She described it as *'quite ancient and an absolute horror!'*[12]

The last week in each category was devoted to a complete revision of the course, followed by the final examinations which involved written, oral and practical tests. Many of the girls remember that after qualifying, they found themselves embroidering their own category (or trade) badges, as the official ones were not available! Skills with the needle were also useful at other times as, generally, the girls worked in bellbottoms, seamens' jerseys, navy shirts and overalls - none exactly designed with the female in mind! Going ashore uniform included a raincoat and greatcoat. Many Wrens recall the amount of sewing to shorten raincoats, or make bellbottoms less cumbersome.

Extensive use was made of modern teaching aids at HMS Fledgling including educational films. In addition, for practical experience, the establishment had a small fleet of aircraft for ground handling and other exercises. These included a Corsair, a Wildcat, a Fulmar, a Blackburn Shark, a Swordfish, a Walrus, an Anson, a Hurricane, and a Percival Proctor. It is curious to note that whilst the area in which the hangars were situated, and the aircraft were used, was referred to as *'the airfield'*, HMS Fledgling had no runway. No flights were made in or out of the base. All aircraft were transported in or out of the establishment by road.

Fledgling's instructors included staff from the *'parent'* establishment HMS

Towing aircraft HMS Fledgling.

Daedalus II, travelling in from Newcastle-under-Lyme as required. These highly experienced personnel, specialists in their fields, had worked their way up from the lower deck. Some were doing shore duty after lengthy spells at sea, whilst others had been recalled to the colours. Previously responsible for training hundreds of men, some admitted that they were not looking forward to training girls! Among the instructors was former PO Air Mechanic (E) W. J. Churchouse who recalled the strict rules regarding *'handling'* of the Wrens and forbidding relationships. He remembers an occasion when a male colleague was seen to be sitting holding hands with a Wren on one of the station's grassed areas. A few days later, he was drafted to sea! There were also occasions when a duty PO would be instructed to drill a squad of Wrens, or take them on a march along the lanes in the vicinity. On returning to base fellow instructors, aware of this, would sometimes quip - *'you're walking rather queer!'*[13]

For all their misgivings, a few months after commissioning, the instructors were reported to be *'all enthusiastic over the results they were getting, and the attitude of the girls to their work.'* The writer of a surprisingly revealing magazine article for the period, seemingly uncensored, wrote that, having visited HMS Fledgling, he or she gained the impression that *'a high percentage'* of girls would pass out as Air Mechanics, also commenting that *'the Navy's new venture should be a success and a real asset to the Air Branch.'*[14]

Figures in relation to the number of trainees and their success rate at HMS Fledgling are difficult to come by, assuming that they existed. After all, there was a war on! However, M.H. Fletcher states that the peak number attending the establishment in 1944 was 1,581.[15] Those who successfully completed the course and *'passed out'*, were then likely to be drafted to naval air stations such as HMS Daedalus at Lee-on -Solent, or HMS Blackcap.

## NOTES

1  Betty Finn. Letter to author February 1997 (undated)
2  The Aeroplane op.cit
3  Ministry of Information Fleet Air Arm (HMSO 1943) p37
4  Ibid
5  Pam Lawler. Letters to author 3 & ll June 1997
6  Eileen Smith. Letter to author 3 February 1997
7  Betty Finn. op.cit
8  Jean Margaret Sole. Letter to author 25 June 1997
9  Helen T. Proctor. Letter to author 23 June 1997
10  Jean Williams. Letter to author 26 July 1997
11  Joan Garvey. Letter to author 4 June 1997
12  Margaret Tansey. Letters to author 17 July & 17 August 1997 - see also Women in Uniform 1939-45 by Jane Waller & Michael Vaughan-Rees (Papermac 1989) p29
13  W.J. Churchouse. Letter to author April 1997 (undated)
14  The Aeroplane op.cit
15  The WRNS by M.H. Fletcher (Batsford 1989) p. 61

Wrens at HMS Fledgling, Mill Meece, 1943.

*Courtesy of Betty Finn*

Wrens learning about the intricacies of the Barracuda engine, HMS Fledgling 1944.

*Courtesy of Helen Proctor*

*Courtesy of Helen Proctor*

A number of Air Mech. Class E18 with accommodation hut in the background.
HMS Fledgling 1944.

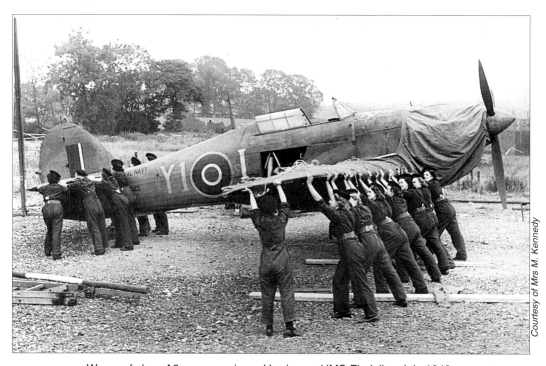

*Courtesy of Mrs M. Kennedy*

Wrens of class A2 manoeuvring a Hurricane, HMS Fledgling July 1943.

Courtesy of Margaret Tansey

Class L 28, HMS Fledgling, with C.O. Captain Percival, centre and instructors. 1944.

*Courtesy of May Calvert*

Handling a Percival Proctor, HMS Fledgling, July 1943.

Wrens from Class 01 with instructors after passing out at HMS Fledgling, Sept 1943.
Mrs Pam Lawler who supplied the photo is 2nd from right, middle row.

Wrens of the Air Mechanic 04 Class, HMS Fledgling, Dec 1943. CPO Tim Gavin is standing end left, second row. Wren Eileen Keefe (now Smith), who supplied the photo, is seated fourth from the left.

*Courtesy of Mrs M. Kennedy*

Wrens of Class A2 with instructors, HMS Fledgiling, July 1943.

Class E12, HMS Fledgling, with instructors. Wren 3rd Officer B.W. Pellow is front row centre. Jean Williams who supplied the photo is third from the right, back row. Jan 1944.

*Courtesy of Betty Finn*

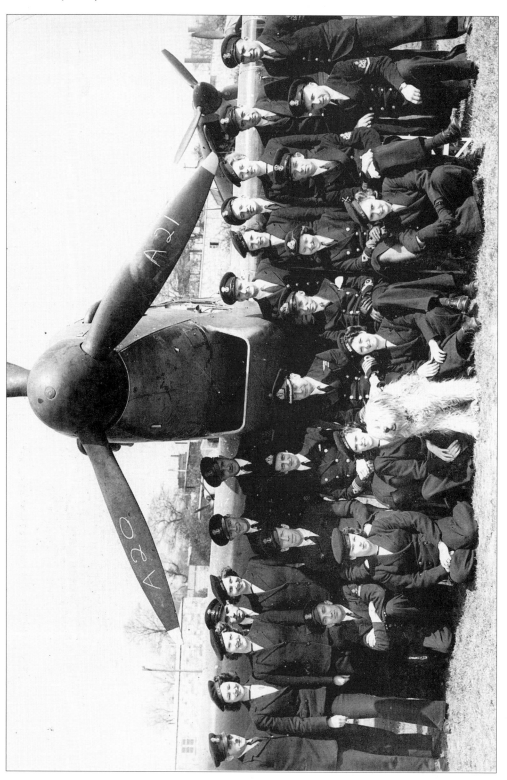

Airframe Mechanic Classes A20 and A21 with instructors, HMS Fledgling, 1943.
Capt Percival is seen centre with his old English sheepdog.

# CHAPTER 6

# NAUTICAL RECREATION

*'We were taken on a visit to the Wedgwood factory and also to a training coal mine on the outskirts of Stoke-on-Trent - all fascinating stuff'*
Former PO Wren Air Fitter (E) Jean Williams (nee Webb)[1]

Surprisingly, perhaps, the social life of North Staffordshire during World War II has been described as 'pretty hectic' by some of those who experienced it. The reasons for this can be attributed to the presence of vast numbers of female workers, being away from home, who were employed locally in the munitions and other factories, plus the ranks of armed forces personnel stationed in the area. Many can recall being caught up in the wonderful atmosphere and have fond memories of dances and other social events at the Municipal Hall and Castle Hotel, Newcastle-under-Lyme; Lewis's, Hanley; the King's Hall in Stoke-on-Trent; Trentham Gardens; and the Borough Hall, Stafford. Whilst the Fledgling personnel who could afford it frequented these venues, they also had the benefit of being able to attend locally organised functions at the adjacent Royal Ordnance Factory's halls of residence where there always seemed to be some form of entertainment provided. Indeed, the factory workers organised a remarkable social life for themselves, but were prepared to share it with others. Consequently, there was a constant stream of dances, film shows, pageants, talent shows, gramophone concerts etc for the taking.

Not to be outdone, the Fledgling personnel contributed in no small way to the social scene themselves. There was a wealth of talent amongst the ranks of the crew - singers, dancers, instrumentalists, and this revealed itself in shows that were staged on board or, on occasion, at other venues in the district. Many of the performances were organised by CPO Tim Gavin, an instructor from HMS Daedalus II. Of all those who served at the two training establishments, the name of Tim Gavin stands out more than any other as one who set out to enrich the social life of service personnel in North Staffordshire. The popular and

*I know I put my identity book* somewhere."

Courtesy of Ken Gavin

CPO Tim Gavin who did so much to enrich the social life of those serving on HMS Fledgling and HMS Daedalus during World War II.

highly respected officer is fondly remembered, not only for his teaching skills, but also for his contribution to entertainment in the area during the dark days of the war.

Betty Finn was a member of a concert party at HMS Fledgling during her period of training. She and her colleague, Gladys Ellis, choreographed the shows and were also members of the chorus line. For one production, she recalls, the Wren Officers cleverly improvised can-can outfits from black-out material and bandages![2] Jean Williams also fondly remembers the *'excellent'* shows by the ship's concert party, appropriately called *Going Astern*. She also recalls the ENSA (Entertainments National Service Association - also sometimes unkindly referred to as 'Every Night Something Awful!') concerts being held on board and in

Courtesy of Betty Finn

The 1943 Ship's concert was choreographed by Betty Finn (right) and Gladys Ellis.

Courtesy of Dorothy Oates

A chorus line of wrens from HMS Fledgling, in one of the many shows they organised.

the area.[3] In addition, parties and entertainment were provided locally at the Front Line Club, Stone Road, Eccleshall.[4]

For the more culturally inclined, there were concerts at the Victoria Hall, Hanley. Regularly, the Halle Orchestra under the baton of Sir John Barbirolli, and the Liverpool Philharmonic conducted by Dr (later Sir) Malcolm Sargeant were in attendance. There was also no shortage of first class artistes appearing locally during the war period including the likes of Joan Hammond (soprano), Heddle Nash (tenor), Gladys Ripley (contralto), and Kathleen Ferrier (contralto). In addition, the Hanley venue played host to the great jazz stars of the era including Nat Gonella, and provided other popular forms of entertainment such as wrestling. Likewise, Stafford's Borough Hall featured concerts by the Halle and the City of Birmingham Symphony Orchestra under George Weldon. Supporting artistes there included Isobel Baillie (soprano) and pianists Eileen Joyce and Solomon. Some were attracted to music for the first time, the concerts providing a form of escapism during the dark years of the war.

Cinemas too were a popular source of entertainment. Newcastle-under-Lyme alone boasted four, but there were also 'picture-palaces' in Hanley, Stoke-on-Trent, Stone, and Stafford , all within reach of the Fledgling personnel, particularly at weekends. At such times, many of the Wrens visited Hanley, taking the opportunity to visit a hairdresser, tour the shops, have a snack at the YWCA or other service personnel centre, and then go to the cinema.

The newcomers also came to appreciate the Staffordshire countryside, sentiments which many have retained. The cycle was a popular form of transport and some of the Wrens would not only use them to tour the leafy country lanes in the vicinity, but also to reach Stafford and Newcastle-under-Lyme. Otherwise, the nearby towns were accessible by public transport. Jean Williams recalls 'a very ancient bus which provided a service into Eccleshall - 4d each way, generally overworked and overloaded, with an elderly driver and conductor.'[5] The area also provided opportunities for walking, and this activity was very popular, particularly in the Summer. Visits to local factories and potbanks such as Josiah Wedgwood & Sons Ltd., were also arranged. Some recall visiting the Etruria factory and being fascinated at the various manufacturing processes involved, particularly the hand-painting of ware.

Sleeping out passes (SOPs) were available monthly, and there were those like Pam Lawler who hitched rides on those weekends to Birmingham, Chester and Manchester. Not really having had an opportunity to travel before, the Wrens decided to visit the bigger cities while they had an opportunity to do so. Many were shocked, however, at the real life scenes of devastation following enemy bombing raids.

Others can recall pleasant evenings at local hostelries - the Duke of York at Mill Meece, and the Cock Inn, Stableford. Generally, however, use of public houses was restricted to officers and ship's company, such premises being placed out of bounds to Wren trainees. Former PO Air Mechanic (E) W.J. Churchouse recalls the 'black out' arrangements at the Duke of York which included 'a large brown blanket fixed over the entrance.'[6]

Sporting activities were organised for the trainees and included netball, hockey, lacrosse, and tennis. Personnel from HMS Fledgling were also allowed free use of a grass tennis court at nearby Mill Meece Farm, on condition that they maintained it. The Bennison family at the farm also loaned a piano to the Officers' Mess. Indeed, there was an excellent relationship formed between the family and the ship's crew which was to the benefit of all concerned. Officers and ratings were frequently entertained at the farm and in return, 'for services rendered,' honorary membership of the Officers' Ward Room was conferred on Mr Bennison. The establishment also supplied the farm with daily leftovers from the messrooms for use as pig swill, and Wrens helped with harvesting at the farm, and others in the area.[7] A number recall volunteering to help in the fields with harvesting, describing it as *'great fun'*. In turn, their help was very much appreciated by the local community. But, in any event, the girls appear to have enjoyed the experience, pleased also to be able to leave their studies and be out in the fresh air and sun, if only temporarily. Pam Lawler remembers that they were rewarded for their efforts with some *'home made eats'* which resulted in the work being 'all the more enjoyable.'[8] Former Second Officer Wren Audrey Deacon shared this view, explaining in her diary that the scheme was that *'under which one offered one's doubtfully valuable services to farmers in view of the shortage of labour'*. She also found the experience *'very pleasant'*, adding *'the sun is lovely if one isn't in uniform!'*[9] Jean Williams also has fond memories of visiting the church in Eccleshall to admire the harvest festival decorations - *'huge marrows and pumpkins among other fruits and bread etc.'*[10]

For many, despite the war, the highlight of the year was the Christmas festivities, no matter where they were. This meant that the horrors of the conflict could be disregarded, if only temporarily. Anyone not having served in HM. Forces may not appreciate that yuletide celebrations can be slightly different from those at home, following certain age old customs such as officers serving lower ranks at meal times. Fortunately, a contemporary record of Christmas 1943 at HMS Fledgling, as seen through the eyes of one young Wren trainee, has survived. On Boxing Day, she wrote to her parents of the 'gorgeous' Christmas dinner consisting of *'lovely turkey, ham, sausage, stuffing, Brussels sprouts, & baked potatoes followed by Christmas pudding and custard.'* But, she wrote, *'that was mere detail compared to the goings-on during dinner!'* After the Captain and Chief Officer had visited, she explained that 'all the Wren PO's served us *'dressed in a marvellous travesty of uniforms with feathers, aprons and rouge all over themselves'*. They bellowed *'any complaints?'* into a megaphone, to which everyone shrieked *'no!'* Later some PO's entered resplendent in borrowed officers' suits, some wearing wigs, and proceeded to *'do impressions of everyone'* whilst standing on tables. Afterwards the correspondent and her colleagues were *'simply too weak to finish their dinner with laughing and wept quietly into their plates.'* *'Very funny'* she added. Then, at the end of the day, *'a remarkably drunk'* Wren PO got *'quite tangled up'* by announcing *'Lights down - pipe out'* instead of *'Lights out - pipe down!'* By this time, she wrote, *'we were in a very reduced state owing to so much laughing!'*[11]

Meanwhile, on the war front in that year, the Italians had earlier surrendered following the capture of Sicily. Also, one thousand Allied aircraft had unleashed two thousand tons of bombs on Frankfurt, Mannheim, and other industrial cities in southern Germany. On the day that the young Wren had written her letter, referred to in the previous paragraph, the sinking of the German battle cruiser Scharnhorst had been announced, resulting in the end of the German High Seas Fleet. Three days later, another two thousand, three hundred tons of bombs relentlessly rained down on Berlin, making a total of fourteen thousand tons in the last six weeks. Victory, at last, seemed to be within our grasp, but at what price?

NOTES

1    Jean Willams. Letter to author 26 July 1997
2    Betty Finn. Letters to author 1997 (undated) and 20 February 2000
3    Jean Williams. op.cit
4    Staffordshire Advertiser 12 January 1945
5    Jean Williams. op.cit
6    W.J. Churchouse op.cit

7 John Bennison Snr. Interview with author 3 March 1997
8 Pam Lawler. Letter to author 11 June 1997
9 Mrs A.D.Deacon. op.cit p171
10 Jean Williams op.cit
11 Jean Williams. Letter to her parents 26 December 1943 (copy in author's collection)

A group of Wrens from HMS Fledgling taken on a visit to
the Wedgwood factory at Etruria. 1943.
Wren Amy Herbert (Mansfield), who supplied the photo, is left foreground.

Courtesy of Betty Finn

HMS Fledgling concert in 1943 organised and performed by the Ship's crew.

## PROGRAMME

1. OVERTURE
2. MEET THE BOYS and GIRLS — The Chorus and the "Gang"
3. AN AUDITION — Joe Riley
4. TWO SONGS — Joyce Wainwright
5. HAPPY HARMONIES — Fred Brunger
6. A FLEDGLING STORY — Johnny Welham
7. ON THE STRAIGHT SIDE — Dennis Popplewell
8. IT'S FOOLISH-BUT IT'S FUN — Jo Robertson, Margaret Needham
9. FANTASY — Waltz of the Flowers, Nutcracker Suite — The Chorus

— *INTERVAL* —
*(If you have to go out make sure your journey is really necessary)*

10. SOUTH AMERICAN WAY — Tommy - Margery Dugard — Dennis Popplewell and Chorus
11. JOYCE AGAIN — Joyce Wainwright
12. MERRY MELODIES — Fred Brunger
13. DUET — Isabel Steel, Ann Annable
14. A CHANGE IN MOOD — Dennis Popplewell
15. THE ARTIST — Joe Riley, Johnny Welham, June Barber-Starkey
16. SOMEDAY — Cliff Thompson
17. PEP ON THE KEYS
18. THE SWINGING DOORS — Clark's Canadian Clowns
19. TORRID TEMPO — Red Pitkin, Beryl Holloway & the Chorus
20. THE BOYS and GIRLS SAY GOODNIGHT

*THE KING*

THE CHORUS :- Paddy Larkin, Dot Aspin, Margery Dugard, Joan Harris, Beryl Holloway, Margaret Smith, Pauline Gibbs, Kay Mitchell.

THE GANG :- Ralph Wallace, Don Jackson, Abie Dean, Red Pitkin, Erland Smith.

CLARKS CLOWNS :- You know them better than we do !

DANCES :- Devised and Directed by Ch/Officer Drummond.

BAND :- Under the direction of Stan Pepper.

ACCOMPANISTS :- Stan Pepper and Betty Richards.

STAGE MANAGERS and LIGHTING EFFECTS :- Ron Batten and Arthur Cobbett.

ASSISTANTS :- R. Gilmour and W. Goyne.

MAKE-UP :- 3rd. Officer Mac Callum, Mary Taylor and Vi Osman.

DRESSES :- 3rd. Officer Mac Callum, Paddy Larkin and P.O. Whitehouse.

SOMEDAY :- Music by Stan Pepper. Lyrics by Cliff Thompson.

*Please do not eat chips during the show or park your gun under the seats.*

PROGRAMME PRICE :- How much have you got ?

THE
MILL MEECE
MANIACS

present

# "PANDEMONIUM"

ON

## TUESDAY and WEDNESDAY

February 6th and 7th 1945.

AT

2000 hours.

IN

## PEREGRINE THEATRE

Proceeds in aid of the RED CROSS P.O.W. Fund.

*H.M.S. "Fledgling"*

*Christmas 1944.*

*The Captain and Officers extend to all present*
*Best Wishes for a Merry Christmas.*

## CHRISTMAS DINNER.

### TOASTS.

1.   THE KING.
Proposed by Stoker R. Blaikie R.C.N.V.R.

2.   THE CAPTAIN.
Proposed by Able Seaman G. A. Murray R.N.

SPEECHES by :-

| | | |
|---|---|---|
| Air Mechanic | J. Kelly | R.N. |
| Stoker | D. Jackson | R.C.N.V.R. |
| Wren | C. H. Saunders | W.R.N.S. |

### SING SONG.

# CHAPTER 7

# YANKS

*'British women have proved themselves in this war.... There isn't a single record of any British woman in uniformed service quitting her post, or failing in her duty under fire. When you see a girl in uniform with a bit of ribbon on her tunic, remember she didn't get it for knitting more socks than anyone else in Ipswich.'*

Extract from US War Department booklet issued to
all American servicemen entering Britain

With the arrival of American troops in the United Kingdom, the social life of North Staffordshire was further enhanced and, in some ways, took on a whole new meaning! The first US. servicemen arrived in Britain in early 1942. By May 1944, there were one and half million American soldiers, sailors and airmen stationed here, poised to assist in the launch of an allied offensive on Hitler's 'Fortress Europe'. It was a colossal build up with Americans seemingly everywhere. Convoys of transport whined through the blacked-out streets, and the country's dance halls and pubs appeared to be full of American uniforms.

It is difficult to confirm precisely when the US. servicemen arrived in the Swynnerton, Cotes Heath and Yarnfield areas, as times being what they were, their arrival is unlikely to have been heralded in the media. Nevertheless, some indication may be gleaned from the records of the former Stone Rural District Council, where the first references to American servicemen may be found in the minutes of a meeting held on 26th October 1943. These reveal that, due to the numbers of troops at Howard, Beatty, Duncan and Nelson Halls, the local authority was experiencing difficulty in coping with the increased level of refuse collections. However, following requests, assistance was provided to the Council in the form of US. transport.[1]  Problems also occurred subsequently, following a number of attempts by American servicemen to dispose of live ammunition in the refuse collections. This resulted in a number of explosions at Council waste tips following fires. The Police were notified and, as a precaution, the public were advised not to trespass onto the authority's disposal sites.[2]

Most British people had not encountered real live Americans before the arrival of US. troops. As Juliet Gardiner observed - *'their image had been shaped by weekly visits to the cinema where America was depicted as a land of chromium plated sophistication and wealth, if it wasn't the Wild West!'*[3] At that time, the average weekly pay of US. privates and corporals was nearly five times that of their British counterparts. This was largely spent on girls, drink, cigarettes, and entertainment - not necessarily in that order! In addition, they could purchase goods, including food, at their PX establishments (equivalent of NAAFIs) at subsidised prices. Apart from the financial aspect, certain other factors proved to be an attraction to some of the British girls. The Americans used deodorants and aftershaves, cosmetic items completely unknown to British men at the time. Former Wren Eileen Smith (nee Keefe) attended the Air Mechanic 'O' 4 course at HMS Fledgling from July to December 1943, and she remembers the arrival of American troops in the locality. *'They soon discovered where we were'* she recalled, *'and they began to show up outside the camp's security fence.'* At the same time, some began to question whether locating large numbers of US. servicemen so close to a camp full of girls was a wise decision, and simply asking for trouble! Eileen gained the impression that the Americans must have thought that the Wrens were *'poor little inmates of some kind, because they brought all kinds of toiletries that we hadn't seen since the beginning of the war, and threw them over the fence to us!'*[4] Otherwise, at this period, without such refinements, some women were driven to using cooked beetroot juice for lipstick and soot for eye make-up. Also, gravy browning *'paint'* was a substitute for silk stockings with pencilled-in seams. Early in the war it was generally considered unpatriotic for women to wear make-up, but they soon came to realise that looking good helped to boost morale, and that fashion aids such as a little make-up and jewellery were the best ways to liven up some of the drab outfits they were being forced to wear because of war-time restrictions. Even the commercial use of silk for women's stockings and underwear was banned to reserve supplies for the manufacture of parachutes. However, the Americans seemed to have access to endless supplies of nylons and other items of lingerie!

To the young men of Britain, whether in uniform or otherwise, the American troops were seen as a threat, and whenever tensions flared up between the two, the disagreements were generally about girls, or perhaps merely due to too much alcohol. Much drunkenness was reported among the US. servicemen, particularly in the Manchester and Liverpool areas where it was not unknown for them to drink a pub dry.[5] In Newcastle-under-Lyme there was a period when there were frequent 'battles' between Americans and Fleet Air Arm apprentices from HMS Daedalus II. These usually commenced at a public house on the outskirts, and then continued up into the town centre by which time the two sides would be fighting with bricks,

Top: US troops on parade in Stafford.
Middle: The US Forces Motor Pool at Duncan Hall.
Bottom: The US Forces' Chapel at Duncan Hall.

The Labour in Vain pub, Yarnfield. A venue frequented by American service personnel.

bottles, and just about everything which came to hand. On most occasions, peace was only restored with the arrival on the scene of both American Military and RN police patrols. For their part, the American Military Police - the notorious 'Snowdrops'- were renowned for their use (or misuse!) of batons and, generally, one did not argue with these. Sometimes the fracas was so serious that the incidents resulted in participants being hospitalised, and also certain hostelries being declared out of bounds for periods.[6]

Sometimes, misunderstandings could arise merely as a result of differences in the meaning of language. Dependent on the circumstances, fighting could result. A completely different example of a misunderstanding was recalled by former Third Officer Wren Rangeley Shallis, Secretary to Fledgling's Chief Officer. On one occasion, when queueing at the local railway station, an American soldier was overheard requesting *'a one way railroad ticket to Axford'*. The booking clerk could not understand him, and was also unable to identify any destination of that name. It was only after others attempted to assist with translation that it transpired that the intended destination was, in fact, Oxford!

To the children of North Staffordshire, the presence of American servicemen meant something else - they were regarded as a walking confectioners, as most were exceedingly generous. Cries of *'got any gum, chum?'* would frequently greet the Americans whenever they appeared on the street, and few could resist the children's eager faces and appeals. Often, packets of gum, chocolates or sweets, and even money, were donated, making the child believe that Christmas had arrived early. On occasions, it was also not unknown for the US servicemen to leave a jeep unattended, and daring youngsters would raid the open vehicle for

The American 'PX' at Howard Hall.

gum etc only to find a loaded service revolver in the glove compartment! These vehicles were often driven with one large combat boot leisurely hanging over the side, and sometimes even on the correct side of the road!

The arrival of the American troops also meant the availability of extra dance venues, as most units organised their own functions. Amongst others, Wrens from HMS Fledgling and HMS Daedalus II were invited to attend on such occasions, and transport would be provided by the hosts. These US transport vehicles became known as 'liberty buses' or 'passion wagons!' Whilst many of the American units had excellent dance bands comprised of instrumentalists from within their own ranks, guest bands, some of them famous, were brought in at times. Some people claim that the legendary Glenn Miller played at Nelson Hall and the ROF, Swynnerton, although this appears to be disputed by music historians. Nevertheless, some insist that they were present when Miller and his band appeared and, times being what they were, it would not be surprising to find that some of these reports were, indeed, correct. After all, it was not unknown for artistes to put in 'surprise' appearances, having been hurriedly slotted into a flexible touring programme to boost morale. Sadly, Miller disappeared whilst on an ill-fated flight from England to France on 15th December 1944. To this day, there remains much speculation about his disappearance. In addition to the Nelson Hall dances, some Wrens recall attending functions at Keele Hall and Crewe Hall where American units were also based. Not to be outdone, the Stafford Civil Defence Service also began organising its own local events. These were generally held in the town's Borough Hall and often featured the dance band from the locally based 16 MU, RAF Stafford, plus the Roosters' Concert Party.[7]

US troops preparing to board coaches at Cold Meece.

Later on, as the war progressed, the Americans became more versatile in providing entertainment and were prepared to show off their talents to the civilian population. Stafford audiences first welcomed a US Army Negro Choir in a concert under the direction of Lt. Ben Suchoff, appearing by permission of Colonel E.C. Humphrey. A local RAF orchestra also shared the programme, and the press reported that *'it was the first occasion that Stafford had been honoured by a joint event given by British and US.Forces'*. The concert was attended by Stafford's Mayor, Councillor H. Wallace Copeland, who commented that *'he had never seen the Borough Hall so full before.'*[8] Ben Suchoff went on to provide further concerts in the town including the popular *Harlem Express* - an all American revue given by US. Army Engineers.[9] Such events provided a welcome diversion which, together with other social activities, were guaranteed to lift spirits and boost morale in the dark days of the war.

Among the locally based American units was the Army Distribution Center (sic) - ADC - whose function was to assign newly arrived air crew to US Bomber Groups, replacing those killed or missing in action. For a brief period, its personnel included 2nd Lt John Howard, a navigator in the Army Air Corps. He and his colleagues had brought in a brand new B-17G bomber across the Atlantic via Prestwick to Warton, north of Liverpool. Shortly afterwards, he and fellow members of his crew were drafted to the ADC near Stone. As a result, John spent the Christmas of 1943 in North Staffordshire and, thankfully, his account of the period survives, providing an excellent record of his activities and also his impressions of the area and its residents. He recalls Christmas Day was spent at the ADC where *'the cooks had done their best to provide us with the military version of a*

US service personnel sounding retreat at Duncan Hall.

*Christmas dinner and all the trimmings.'* 'However, the atmosphere was subdued, with noise and chatter missing as the personnel went through the motions of eating the traditional turkey, stuffing and cranberry sauce. No doubt many were lost in thoughts of their families, friends and loved ones back home,' he contemplated. Later in the day he and his pilot, 2nd Lt Jim Tyson, walked the four miles into Stone - *'its tranquil nature being a sharp contrast to the kaleidoscope of rapid fire events we had been living through'* he wrote. Here they were approached by a middle aged woman and a boy who said - *'won't you Yanks come home and have Christmas tea with us?'* Although somewhat surprised, they nevertheless were quick to accept the offer and joined the family at their home which was already full of people on their arrival. He discovered that the residence was the home of the Redman family, the head of the household being a director of the famous locally based Joules brewery. John wrote that he and his colleague wondered *'where to find the 'cold' and 'aloof' English people they had heard so much about'*. Whilst with their hosts conversation flowed freely, the tea and scones were delicious, and they had been treated with *'a warmth and friendship'* they had not encountered since leaving home.

On returning to the base, John learned that fellow crew member 2nd Lt Frank Palenk and a friend had also shared a similar experience. They had met a young girl in Stone who had invited them to her home where they were greeted with the words - *'Welcome gentlemen, there is room for you at our inn'*. The residence was the home of the Phillips family who invited them to stay for their traditional Christmas

Eve dinner. However, both Americans being aware of the severe rationing situation, voiced their objections to imposing on the family's hospitality. Nonetheless, their hosts were most insistent and so they agreed to stay. After the meal, Mr Phillips, who turned out to be the town constable, opened a bottle of Scotch whisky, low in content and comfortably aged, which had been purchased some years earlier, and proceeded to pour *'a wee dram'* for each man present. All then shared in the toast - *'peace, harmony and goodwill towards men.'* Subsequently, in relating the experience to his colleagues, Frank spoke of *'the kind and loving people of Stone'* and *'how they shared their scarce treasures with us.'* *'We found common ties spanning thousands of miles we never dreamed existed,'* adding *'it was the most forthright expression of Christmas love and compassion for mankind I have ever received.'*

*Courtesy of The Sentinel*

US soldiers of 2nd Division Service Corps Combat Infantry at Trentham Gardens, 1944.

On 27th December, John Howland and fellow members of his crew received orders to join 535 Squadron of the 381st Bomber Group at Ridgewell, East Anglia.[10]

Meanwhile, across the water, the Canadian Government, already involved in escorting Atlantic convoys, had made the decision to form a Naval Air Service to benefit such operations. Strange as it may seem, this decision was to have implications for HMS Fledgling.

NOTES

1    Minutes of Scavenging & Salvage Committee Stone RDC. 26 October 1943 & 14 August 1944
2    Ibid. 11 January 1945
3    Juliet Gardiner. *Over Here - the GI's in Wartime Britain* (Collis & Brown) p111
4    Eileen Smith. Letter to author 3 February 1999
5    Juliet Gardiner. op.cit p80
6    Graham Bebbington. *Ship Without Water* (Churnet Valley Books, Leek) p66
7    Staffordshire Chronicle (various)
8    Ibid. 10 March 1945
9    Ibid. 24 March 1945
10   John W. Howland. *The Class of '43* (Watchman Office Supply) US 1993. pp 40-44

# CHAPTER 8

# 'BIG DADDY' & THE CANADIANS

*'Mill Meece was, and always will be, a special place to me'*
Don Field[1]

Whilst Canada was involved with naval aviation operations during World War I, the Dominion did not possess an Air Arm when it entered World War II. Nevertheless, within a short time, highly placed officials of the Royal Canadian Navy (RCN) began to appreciate that deployment of carrier-borne aircraft was becoming crucial to the successful prosecution of war at sea.

Thus, after deliberations between Canadian officials and the Admiralty in London, two escort carriers were made available to the Dominion and commenced operations in European waters. HMS Pincher and HMS Nabob were Royal Naval vessels, acquired from the United States on the so called 'lend-lease' scheme, and manned by Canadian officers and crew. However, the aviation personnel were British.

The Dominion's naval aviation plans continued to develop when Captain H.N. Lay RCN, Director of Operations Division at Naval HQ, Ottawa was appointed to undertake a comprehensive study of United Kingdom and United States naval air operations. But, according to Peter Charlton & Michael Whitby, even before Lay's report was submitted, Ottawa had directed the Senior Canadian Naval Officer in London to arrange for the training of pilots, observers, air gunners and air maintenance artificers by the Royal Navy. At a meeting on 13th August 1943, a group of British and Canadian naval officials, including Captain Lay, began discussions with a view to developing a training scheme. Eventually, on 31st July 1944, a programme was finalised that would generate five hundred and twenty nine qualified air maintenance fitters.[2] By this time, it had also been learned that two UK bases could be made available, and they were understood to be 'perfect' for Canadian training requirements. Both HMS Turnstone, Watford and HMS Fledgling, Mill Meece had instructors in place with ships' companies, and facilities to house students. HMS Turnstone was to be used for initial training, aptitude tests and classification of trade (ie. engines, airframes, electronics or ordnance) before transferring personnel to HMS Fledgling for designated trade instruction. In the meantime, volunteers had been sought from the RCN's stoker and seaman branches, and the initial draft of air mechanic trainees arrived in Britain on 13th August 1944.[3]

The young Canadians arrived at Watford via various routes, having crossed the Atlantic in such vessels as the RMS Queen Mary and the Ile de France, converted from luxury liners for troop carrying operations. Dave Conkie recalled that quartering on the Ile de France was tight, although he and his colleagues were in first class accommodation! Thirty two were housed in a cabin, utilising eight tiers of bunks. Consequently, it was impossible for more than three or four to rise at one time![4] Thankfully, all arrived safely having avoided the threat of the menacing German 'U' boats.

At Watford, they were met by Lt. Don W. Clark RCN who explained, in the course of his welcome, the volume and extent of the aptitude tests that they were to undergo at HMS Turnstone, the results of which would determine their future in the service. Don Clark was to fill an important role in the lives of his young fellow countrymen, acting as Canadian Liaison Officer, travelling from station to station by motorcycle, and generally ensuring that there was peace and order among the trainees.

It was during this period, on 17th September 1944, that the famous Operation 'Market Garden' was launched. The Allied Command believed that retreating German forces were so disorganised and demoralised, that a surprise airborne landing could speedily capture intact the many bridges across rivers and canals in Holland. However, German resilience was severely underestimated, and a bitter struggle ensued, particularly at Arnhem. More than thirty five thousand airborne troops were committed, together with four thousand six hundred aircraft and gliders. Some of the Canadians who were present at Watford at the time witnessed part of the 'air armada' on its way. Don Field remembers that he was just returning to the workshops after lunch when he and his colleagues heard 'a very loud roar of aircraft engines.' Looking up, he saw *the sky was filled with cargo planes and gliders for as far as the eye could see!* Of course, Don and his colleagues had no idea then of the purpose or destination of the aircraft but declared that it was a never to be forgotten sight' that would remain with him always. It was a part of history, and he felt 'privileged to have seen it.'[5]

After their brief sojourn at HMS Turnstone, the selected trainees travelled by rail to North Staffordshire, the first contingent arriving at Mill Meece on 18th October 1944.[6] By coincidence, on the day of their arrival, the local Sentinel announced that the Canadian 1st Army had captured the village of Tjzendijke in the Scheldt pocket, but the report added that *every yard of ground was being bitterly contested.* The newspaper also reported that, down in Italy, the North Staffs Regiment was fighting its way through the deep defences of the Gothic Line, north of Florence. However, on a lighter note, the Minister of Food, Colonel Llewellin, had announced plans to fill the nation's Christmas stockings with 'many extras.' For example, there was to be *a turkey for each family that wanted one, extra allowances for meat, sugar and margarine, more dried fruit and nuts, and more sweets for the children!*[7]

Don Field was among the first Canadian arrivals at Mill Meece. A twenty-two year old fromVancouver, he had been selected for training as an engine aero mechanic. His ambition had always been to join the air force, but unfortunately there had been no vacancies at the time that he had applied. Not wishing to be conscripted, Don had volunteered for the CRN. Subsequently, when a chance of joining the then forming Canadian Fleet Air Arm had arisen, he considered it an opportunity not to be missed! Don estimated that there were approximately two hundred Wrens still present at HMS Fledgling on his arrival, including those of the ship's company.[8] With the number gradually reducing as Wrens qualified, their places were taken by Canadian trainees. Wrens included in the ship's company were retained throughout to assist in administering the base, and also to maintain catering and laundering facilities etc. Naturally, Wrens' living quarters were declared out of bounds to the male population but whose membership persistently sought to devise all possible means to circumvent the Regulations, despite regular base patrols!

In general, the Canadians found Fledgling's accommodation to be *'first class.'* Harry Marwood described it as *'something to be seen'* - the mattresses, sheets and bed spreads with a navy anchor in the centre being a far cry from the Canadian naval issue of a swinging hammock and coarse blanket! Being a 'killick' (leading seaman), Don Field shared his accommodation with another colleague, otherwise generally there were four to a room. Having a hot water radiator was also regarded as a luxury as, with winter approaching, there was not only warmth but a facility to dry and air clothing.[9] Messing was in RN tradition with the killick seated at the head of the table, and serving the food. Generally, the standard of food seems to have found favour with the Canadians, and they appear to have had few, if any, complaints. Others appreciated a female presence in the dental surgery in the form of Surgeon Lt (D) Miss M.M. Hunter LDS!

Courses for the Canadians at Mill Meece generally lasted for four months. The period was regarded as *'very intensive'*, being *'busy most of the time in classes or receiving instruction on the aircraft that were there.'* At the same time, trainees came under the influence of Captain Charles Halliwell RM who had been brought out of retirement to aid the war effort. Born in 1897, Halliwell had made his way up through the ranks, his unblemished service record indicating that he had previously been *'a first class Parade Sgt Major, zealous, tactful, loyal and a good disciplinarian.'* *'A fine example to NCOs and men'* it continued, adding *'an exceptionally good instructor. Patient and efficient.'*[10] Few of the Canadians fail to mention Captain Halliwell in recalling their period at HMS Fledgling.

Described as being over six feet in height, Halliwell is said to have *'carried himself with dignity, whilst perhaps being a little overweight.'* Overweight or not, despite the age difference, Halliwell was certainly fitter than the majority of his young and restless charges, as many testify! Reputed also to have attended to his own attire, when in uniform, Halliwell was described as *'spick and span with nothing out of order.'* According to Don Field, the officer was *'a real soldier and held in great respect by all who knew him.'*[11] John Anderson also characterizes the Royal Marine Officer as *'a true gentleman, almost to the point of being gullible to some of our schemes!'*[12] Such terms of endearment no doubt also resulted in him being referred to as 'Pops' or 'Big Daddy' by the Canadians, but certainly not to his face!  Electrician Jim Gilchrist recalls seeing Captain Halliwell in full uniform doing push ups adding - 'he could do more than all of us nineteen or twenty years olds!'[13]  Regularly, he took trainees for an early morning run around the country lanes, he taking the lead *at the double!'*  However, it was not unknown for certain participants to slip from the ranks and nip inside an air raid shelter on a corner on the route.  They would then remain there until the group returned, hopefully rejoining it without Captain Halliwell or any of the accompanying NCOs noticing!  John Callard described the officer as *'the Canadians' father and mother at Fledgling, as we were a lonely, homesick bunch, and he took us under his wing and nurtured us through a scary time.'*[14]

Basically, HMS Fledgling had been organised as *'a new entry unit'* with appropriate rules and regulations.  However, the Canadian trainees were not new entrants, a number of them having been in the service for some time.  Consequently, the strict regime did not, according to John Anderson, *'sit well'* with the Canadians.  For example, a number of his colleagues were ranked Senior A/B's, having been used to all night leave.  The fact that  nightly shore leave at the establishment expired at 1900 hrs, and at midnight during weekends did not find find favour with them.  The Canadians were organised on a four watch system, with colour-watch station cards, but it was not long before a scheme had been devised to circumvent the procedure!  A supply of blank cards was found during fatigue duties in the Regulating Office and John recalls that *'these were forged and put to good use, giving extra leave and time off!'*  Also, a hole in the rear security fence was used at times to abscond temporarily from the base, that is until some Wrens *'squealed'* to the authorities![15]

Like the American servicemen, the Canadians were on higher rates of pay than their British counterparts.  Reminiscing, John Anderson remembers that he and his colleagues could *'fill a table with beer, when RN personnel could only afford to pay for a single pint!'*  Furthermore, the Canadian dollar had been pegged at 4.43 to the pound sterling and, according to John, they found that in some instances, they were drawing more pay than certain British officers!  The higher rate of pay also enabled the Canadians to buy up issues of 'tickler' (tobacco) from their RN colleagues.  The going rate was ten shillings per half pound can, and this could be resold in the Stafford pubs at double the price![16]

North Staffordshire, in common with many other parts of the country, had a white Christmas in 1944, with heavy falls of snow.  Waxing lyrical, a Sentinel reporter described the local scene as *'a mantle of glistening white on trees, hedges, bushes and roof tops, giving a pleasantly seasonal touch.'*  However, the newspaper also reported that no bus services had run, and that fog and frost conditions were too severe on Christmas night for many drivers to risk. Many travellers had found themselves stranded.[17]

Among those stranded were Don Field and fellow Canadian Lloyd Eaton.  Although it had been snowing for some time, since it was Christmas Eve and they were off duty, they decided to take the first *'liberty boat'* into nearby Newcastle-under-Lyme. However, when they eventually came to catch a bus for the return journey to the base, a civilian passing the bus terminus informed them that no services were running. Indeed, by this time, they began to appreciate that *'nothing was moving.'* Fortunately, they were directed to the Regulating Offices of HMS Daedalus II, then situated in Old Bank House, on the High Street. Having explained their circumstances and that they were, in effect, likely to be classed as 'AWOL', a message was telephoned to HMS Fledgling whereupon permission was granted for them to stay overnight in the town. Accommodation was also arranged for them at the local Municipal Hostel (also under the control of Daedalus), where the two spent *'a miserable night sleeping in their uniforms.'* They were wakened the next morning to cries of *'Eggs, real eggs!'* So for breakfast on Christmas morning they were served real eggs - *'probably the first that we had seen for many a day!'* Don recalled. Following breakfast, having thanked their hosts and bade farewell, the two Canadians set out on foot to walk the nine miles or so to Mill Meece. It was still snowing and they were thankful to be wearing their service issue great coats with a high collar. Walking in each other's foot steps through the deep snow, Don remembered the peaceful atmosphere thinking *'that the war had stopped, or so it seemed. Nothing was moving.'* They eventually reached the base at 5.00pm - just in time for the turkey dinner served, as per naval tradition, by the officers. Don naturally remembers that particular occasion every Christmas, believing it to be *'an experience one never forgets.'*[18] However, for those who remained on the base, Christmas 1944 was a good time, Harry Marwood recalls. He particularly remembers a huge party in the recreation hall.[19]

It was during this time that CPO Tim Gavin was also attempting to reach HMS Fledgling. This popular officer, who specialised in armaments and hydraulics, also served at HMS Daedalus II. Unfortunately, due to the extreme wintry conditions, the RN transport in which he was travelling to Mill Meece was unable to complete the journey. Abandoning the vehicle, Tim then set out on foot, walking through the deep snow, in an attempt to reach the base. This he achieved successfully but, due to the condition he was in on arrival, soon contracted pneumonia. According to his family, Tim's health was never the same afterwards, and sadly he died in October 1945.[20]

As is to be expected in the services, physical activity formed part of the training regime for the Canadians. This included football, cross-country running and tug of war but, according to John Anderson, they weren't too successful at cricket![21] P.T classes were also held regularly, particularly early in the mornings, but Captain Halliwell, being the officer and gentleman that he was, would not allow his young charges to perform their exercises in front of, or at the same time as, the Wrens![22]

Keen to socialise when time permitted, the Canadian boys also participated in ship's concerts, assisting as stage hands or performing on stage. Former L/Wren

Beryl Maxwell (nee Holloway) recalls these occasions as *'a great success.'* Showing off her dancing skills, Beryl shared the stage in one show with a young Canadian named 'Red' Raskin, performing a jive which was *'great fun'*. The show later went on to visit a number of local military hospitals to entertain patients and staff.[23]

For the most part, the Canadians remember their time in North Staffordshire and indeed in the United Kingdom, with affection, and regard the period as *'one of the most important in their lives.'* A number recall the Staffordshire countryside as being *'very pleasant'*, although they never really had the opportunity to fully appreciate it or explore it, or to meet local residents. The only time that they went 'ashore', was to dances in Stafford, or to those held nearby at the US base. Sometimes, they would take short cuts to these functions, walking across ploughed fields, guided by the Wrens.

On qualifying at HMS Fledgling, the Canadians were posted to various Fleet Air Arm bases in Scotland for further training and 'work ups.' By the end of the war, three of the four 'Canadianised' operational RN squadrons, destined to form the nucleus of RCN aviation, were in existence - 803 (Fighter) Squadron; and 825 & 826 (TBR or torpedo/bomber/reconnaisance) Squadrons. The fourth, 883 (Fighter) Squadron, was commissioned in September 1945. Eventually, 803 & 825 Squadrons embarked on the newly built carrier HMCS Warrior and sailed for Canada arriving in late March 1946.[24] It is interesting to note that its aircraft also included three machines destined for cold weather testing at Canada's Winter Experimental Establishment (WEE).[25]

Whether or not the target figure for the number of trained Canadian air maintenance fitters was ever achieved is difficult to confirm, but respected local historian Norman Cope claims that 420 qualified at HMS Fledgling.[26]

NOTES

1    Don Field. Letter to author 3 June 1997
2    Peter Charlton & Michael Whitby. Certified Serviceable (Publishing Plus , Ottawa) p14
3    Service record of Don Field (copy in author's collection). The author is also most appreciative of the assistance of members of the Canadian Association Fleet Air Arm Aircrew & the Canadian Naval Air Group for providing additional information.
4    Dave Conkie. Letter to author 10 June 1998
5    Don Field. Letter to author August 1997 (undated)
6    Service record of Don Field.
7    Sentinel 18 October 1944
8    Don Field. Letter to author 19 July 1997
9    Harry K. Marwood. Letter to author 13 January 1999
10   PRO. Ref ADM196/102
11   Don Field. op.cit
12   John Anderson. Letter to author 24 March 1998
13   Jim Gilchrist. Letter to author 16 April 1998
14   John Callard. Letter to author 12 June 1998
15   John Anderson. op.cit

16  Ibid.
17  Sentinel  27 December 1944
18  Don Field. Letter to author 3 June 1997
19  Harry K. Marwood. op.cit
20  Ken Gavin. Letter to author 22 February 1997, and subsequent interviews.
21  John Anderson. op.cit
22  John Callard. op.cit
23  Beryl Maxwell. Letters to author 21 October 1998 & 6 January 2002
24  Peter Charlton & Michael Whitby op.cit  pp12/13
25  Leo Pettipas.  Cold Weather Navy in Jabberwock No.47 Spring 2002
26  Norman A. Cope.  Stone in Staffordshire (Wood, Mitchell & Co.,Hanley) p142

Above:
Canadian Don Field at
HMS Fledgling,
Oct 1944.

Above:
Don Owen and Don
Field, two Canadians at
HMS Fledgling,
October 1944

Left: Beryl Holloway,
HMS Fledgling.

Courtesy of Dorothy Oates

Courtesy of Mrs B. Maxwell

Top: Canadians at stand-easy at HMS Fledgling.

Centre: Wren Val pictured with Canadian servicemen at HMS Fledgling, 1945.

Bottom: Some of the Canadian servicemen seen relaxing outside their accommodation, HMS Fledgling, Feb 1945.

Courtesy of J.A. Gilchrist

Courtesy of Harry Harwood

Canadian ground crew personnel under training early in 1945 at HMS Fledgling.
Instructor RM Capt Charles Halliwell is 2nd left front row, Liaison Officer Don Clark is on his left.

Courtesy of Don Field

The first class of Canadian ground crew to be trained at HMS Fledgling.
Lt. D.W. Clark is seated 2nd from right.
A US Avenger torpedo bomber forms the background.

A number of the Ship's company, HMS Fledgling. Wren Beryl Holloway (Maxwell), who supplied the photo is standing right, middle row.

# The Fledglings

Canadian servicemen of Class L9, HMS Fledgling, Feb 1945. Capt. C. Halliwell, 3rd from left, front row.

*Courtesy of John E. Callard*

Canadian servicemen (Class E5) with Capt. Charles Halliwell RM, and Lts. Mabberley and Clark seated in front.   March 1945.

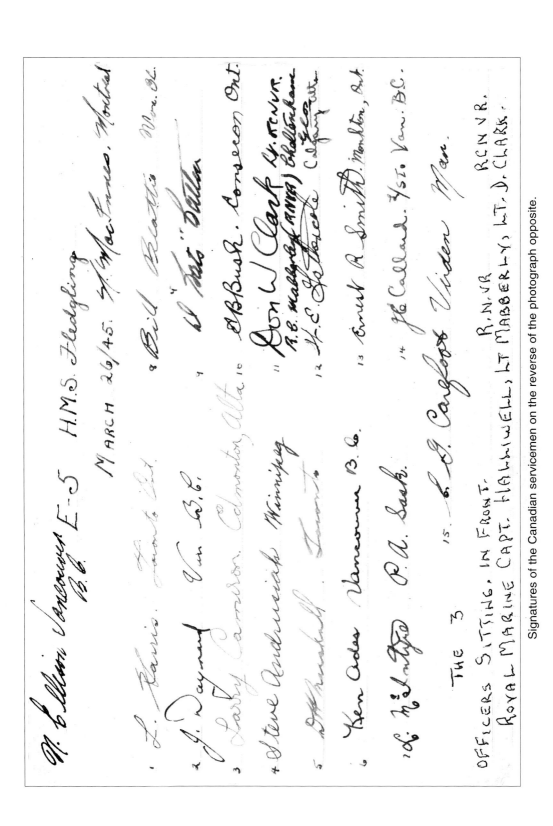

W. Ellison Vancouver E-5 HMS Fledgling
B.C.

MARCH 26/45. S/ MacInnes Montreal

1. L. Harris. Toronto Ont.
2. J. J. Raymond Van. B.C.
3. Larry Cameron. Edmonton, Alta.
4. Steve Andreuiak Winnipeg
5. D. Marshall Toronto.
6. Ken Ades Vancouver B.C.
7. G. Walotyp. P.A. Sask.

8. Bill Beattie Van. B.C.
9. W. "Pete" Butler
10. A.B. Bush. Conneon Ont.
11. Don W. Clark Ty. RCNVR.
R.B. Mabberly ANVA) Belleham
12. H.E. Gotovced Calgary Ont.
13. Ernest R. Smith Moncton, Ont.
14. J. Callard. Van. B.C.
15. L.J. Cargoos Virden Man.

THE 3 OFFICERS SITTING, IN FRONT.
ROYAL MARINE CAPT. HALLIWELL, LT MABBERLY, LT. J. CLARK.
R.N.VR.            RCN VR.

Signatures of the Canadian servicemen on the reverse of the photograph opposite.

A Saturday afternoon in Hanley, summer 1945.
L to R: Tijs Haverkamp, Gerard Mutsaars,
Local girl Ann Pixley and Frans Merkx.

*Courtesy of Gerard Mutsaars*

Dutch personnel under training at HMS Ganges, Shotley (Ipswich),
January 1945, prior to transfer to HMS Fledgling.

# CHAPTER 9

# DUTCH COURAGE

*'Our fleet will rise again, stronger than ever'* Queen Wilhelmina of The Netherlands[1]

On 9th May 1940, the Germans invaded the Netherlands (Holland), Belgium and Luxembourg, crossing their frontiers at numerous points as part of Hitler's western offensive. Fortunately, prior to being seized by the enemy, a number of Dutch naval vessels and crew were able to escape to England where they were placed under British operational orders. Those vessels were -

| | |
|---|---|
| Flotilla leader | Hr. Ms. Jacob van Heemskerk |
| Torpedo boat hunter | Hr. Ms. Issac Sweers. |
| Motor torpedo boat | TM 51 |
| Submarines | O21, O22 & O23 [2] |

A few days later, Fleet Admiral J. Th. Furstner, Commander of the Dutch naval forces, fled to Britain accompanied by several officers, eventually establishing his headquarters at 4 North Row, London. Here, plans immediately began for reinforcing the fleet as, then, a number of vessels remained in the Dutch East Indies. Notwithstanding, these were destined to be destroyed or captured by the Japanese in 1942.

Nevertheless, plans continued for the rebuilding of the fleet, including the question of how it might best be deployed in the war against Japan after the liberation of Holland. It was assumed that the vessels required could be purchased from the Allies, but the subject of manning also arose, and whether conscription might be necessary due to the number of regular personnel, particularly officers, who were prisoners of war in Germany or in the Far East. Furthermore, Dutch airfields and naval bases had been destroyed or plundered by the invading Nazis, leaving no facilities in the Netherlands suitable for training when liberation occurred.

Eventually, on 11th September 1944 Allied forces entered Holland and began liberating the country between the Belgian border and the River Meuse. Shortly afterwards, as part of the naval recruitment strategy, the Law of War Volunteers (E129) was passed on 1st October by the Dutch Government in exile. Apart from those already serving before May 1940, this provided for the voluntary recruitment of males between the ages of 18 - 21 years. So, instead of returning to their former employment and rebuilding their careers, those volunteering put their country first and joined its forces because they were needed. The first applicants under such legislation arrived in Britain for training in December. Fortunately, by this time, the British Royal Navy had also agreed to assist its Dutch colleagues with recruitment and training as part of the general allied war effort.

Gerard Mutsaars was a member of that first draft, his home town of Tilburg having been liberated by the Canadians on 28th October 1944. After reading the notice of appeal for volunteers of war in the newspaper, he signed for service on 10th November.[3] Although a carpenter by trade, what drove him to take such action he explained was *'a mixture of wanting to do something about the situation,a bit of patriotics and seeking adventure after five years of occupation and compulsion.'* Forced by the Germans to become a slaveworker in a coalmine, he had eventually managed to escape and remain in hiding until liberation.

On arrival in England in December, Gerard and his colleagues were initially accommodated on the depot ship 'Oranje Nassau' in the Port of London where they were issued with uniforms and kit. Here, amongst other things, they learned *'the first principles of the ranks'* etc. From there he was drafted to HMS Ganges, Shotley, in Suffolk where initial training was given by Dutch Marines. Having been selected for the Dutch Fleet Air Arm, he was then transferred to HMS Turnstone, Watford to undergo political screening, aptitude tests and theoretical training. Chosen for selection as a trainee Airframe Mechanic, he was then drafted to HMS Fledgling on 2nd July 1945, where training was given by British instructors, assisted by a team of Dutch regulars acting as translators.[4] Here, all trades applicable to the Dutch Fleet Air Arm were trained, with the exception of radio/radar mechanics.

By the time the first group of Dutch servicemen arrived at Mill Meece, a number of Canadians, including John Anderson, remained in training. In recalling the arrival of the Dutch trainees, he recollects that, as with their British counterparts, the Canadians were on higher rates of pay. Accordingly, their dollars had more purchasing power and *'could buy more beer in the canteens.'* Occasionally, there was a little friction between the Canadians and Dutch, mainly perhaps due to language, but the differences were not so serious as those which arose between the British and American servicemen.[5] In contrast, having suffered as they had, Second Officer Wren Audrey Deacon found the young Dutchmen to be *'very light hearted.'* She recalled having working parties of them regularly cleaning her office on Saturday mornings which could prove 'a hilarious experience.' For example, conscious of the approach of noon, when they would normally be off duty, their knowledge of the English language would 'suddenly desert them if they were asked to do anything extra' such as *'Could you polish my desk please?'* This would be met with a response of *'Polish?'* (pronounced as per the nationality!) - *'what is Polish?'*[6] Former L/Wren Dorothy Oates (nee Aspin) concurs with this view. In remembering the Dutch boys with affection, she comments that they *'put us all to shame with their ability to speak English - except when asked to perform certain duties!'* Dorothy adds that they seemed *'so clean, and well behaved. They were all sociable and friendly.'*[7] Mrs M. Collinson, who delivered mail regularly to the naval establishment at the time, also maintains that the Dutch boys were *'very likeable and pleasant.'* She recalls that they spoke a good standard of English, and entered the social scene enthusiastically when they could, attending local dances and other events.[8]

Being young, and having been delivered from years of Nazi oppression, the young Dutch servicemen were naturally keen to socialise, and have some fun and entertainment. Dorothy Oates clearly remembers an incident when, on first arriving, a group of the Dutch boys were sent along to the Victualling Store where she served as a Victualling Supply Wren. Here she instructed them to make some sandwiches for the refreshments for those attending the weekly dance to be held on the base that evening. She recalls - *'they played me up something rotten!'* According to Dorothy, they did eventually complete the task, but thought it most unfair that, for some unknown reason, they were not allowed to attend the function. Dorothy too thought that their exclusion was unmerited, and so a pact was made, agreeing that if they turned up at the venue's stage door at a given hour, she would admit them. Later that evening, the Dutch boys turned up as arranged and were duly admitted. She had *'definitely made friends'* she concluded! Dorothy also recalls lunch times when she and her colleagues would often go to the Wrens' recreation room. Here she would play the piano and, during these sessions, a number of the Dutch boys would sit on the grass outside and listen. On one occasion she was playing *Lili Marlene* when suddenly all her outside audience quickly got up and disappeared. This puzzled her but later, one of the boys came and asked why she had played a German song, since many of them had seen numbers of their families marched away whilst members of the enemy occupying forces had played that tune. That evening, she handed him an envelope in which she had torn the music to shreds. *'They were back on the following day'* she happily recalled![9]

When an opportunity arose, the young Dutch servicemen also liked to visit pubs and cinemas in Stafford and the Potteries towns. With bicycles being a totally accepted mode of personal transport in their own country, the boys also took pleasure in cycling around the country lanes in the vicinity of the naval establishment. Local sporting events were also popular, including football matches, and it was at the former Victoria Ground in Stoke-on-Trent that Gerard Mutsaars recalls seeing the great wizard of dribble, Stanley Matthews (later Sir), in action.[10]

Needless to say, the Dutch did not really have a great deal of time for socialising. They were primarily at HMS Fledgling for the purpose of being trained as ground crew as part of the allied war effort. Like the majority of other trainees who had passed before them at the establishment, they found the courses intensive, using such terms as 'large programme' and 'stiff', but with the added disadvantage of having to learn English. However, classes tended to consist of small numbers which they found to be helpful, not only from a learning aspect, but also appreciating that this could result in promotion being more likely.[11]

Warm friendships built up between the English and the young Dutch sailors - friendships which exist today. Not having homes in this country, they were taken by English friends to spend weekends or longer periods with their families. Gerard Mutsaars was unable to return to the Netherlands until Christmas 1945 and so had not seen his own family for a year. He, in particular, recalls with affection and gratitude, the affinity which grew during his period in Britain, friendships which have lasted over half a century.

Courtesy of Gerard Mutsaars

A class of Dutch aircraft electricians, HMS Fledgling, Summer 1945.
Sitting: Henk Wiltenburg, Leading Air Fitter John Danny,
Frank Rugebregt.
Standing: Piet van Lierop, Jan Hofman, Henny de Klerk.

On qualifying, the Dutch were promoted to Air Mechanic 2nd Class and posted to Fleet Air Arm squadrons in various parts of Britain. The Dutch, at this time, did not have any fighter squadrons in the country, although they did have a bomber squadron (No.320) operating from RAF Dunsfold and RAF Bircham Newton with Hudsons and B25 Mitchells.[12]

During the period that the Dutch were in training in North Staffordshire, incidents happened which, as Gerard Mutsaars rightly states *changed the world forever!*[13] On 2nd August 1945 in the heaviest air raid of the war, 800 US B29 bombers dropped more than 6,000 tons of incendiary bombs on Japanese cities and manufacturing plants. 80,000 people were killed as a result. Four days later, the first atomic bomb, equivalent to 20,000 tons of TNT, was dropped on Hiroshima. From the resultant blast and firestorm, over half the area of the city was laid waste. Some 80,000 were killed, and thousands more maimed and burned. Three days later, a second atomic device was unleashed on Nagasaki killing a further 40,000. This resulted in the final capitulation of Japan. However, the situation had implications for the Dutch volunteers and was to change their destiny, as the terms of their engagement included serving a further six months after the ending of hostilities, that is until the surrender of Japan. Having spent time and money on training, the Dutch authorities were keen to persuade volunteers to sign for a further three years, and large numbers of them did so.

As in the case of earlier trainees, it is extremely difficult to be precise as to the number of Dutch personnel who qualified as Air Mechanics at HMS Fledgling. The situation is further complicated due to a number of Indonesians, as Dutch subjects, who were also in attendance at the time. These were not volunteers, but were already in the navy when the Japanese had attacked the Dutch East Indies. Having

G.T. Mutsaars, Air Mechanic
3rd Class. April 1945.

*Courtesy of Gerard Mutsaars*

Dutch naval personnel under training Summer 1945 at HMS Fledgling.

*Courtesy of Gerard Mutsaars*

British and Dutch air mechanics, HMS Fledgling, Summer 1945.

escaped to Australia, they were shipped to England to complete their training. However, according to Norman Cope, 240 Dutch personnel qualified at the establishment.[14]

Whatever the figure, according to Colonel R.E. van Holst Pellekan, the Dutch volunteers of war were *'a special group in the navy. They were the men who right away after the liberation were willing to take part in the combat in Europe as in the east as well. They did so, taking the consequences of all the risks and leaving their personal interests behind... These were the men who demanded little, were real go-getters and had a great deal of adaptability. They were highly motivated and available for the navy at the moment they were badly needed.'*[15]

## NOTES

1   Taken from a speech given on radio shortly after the Battle of the Java Sea, 27th Feb 1944 when The Netherlands lost most of its Far East Fleet at the hands of the Japanese.
2   Gerard Mutsaars. Letter to author 30 January 1999
3   Signed application form - copy in author's private collection
4   Gerard Mutsaars. Letters to author 14 December 1998 & 9 January 1999
5   John Anderson. op.cit
6   Mrs A.D. Deacon op.cit p170
7   Dorothy Oates. Letter to author 23 January 2002
8   Mrs M.Collinson. Telephone interview with author 21 November 2001
9   Dorothy Oates. Letter to author 20 January 2002
10  Gerard Mutsaars. Letter to author 14 December 1998
11  Gerard Mutsaars. Letter to author 9 January 1999
12  In 1946, the taking over on a temporary basis of RAF Langham, Norfolk, by the Dutch provided an important training centre for the country's Royal Air Force and Fleet Air Arm.
13  Gerard Mutsaars. op.cit
14  Norman A.Cope. op.cit p142
15  Rob.E. van Holst Pellekan. *Tienduizend Vrije Vogels* (De Bataafsche Leeuw, Amsterdam) Translation by G. Mutsaars

*Courtesy of Gerard Mutsaars*

**HOLLANDSCHE JONGENS**
melden zich als
**OORLOGS-VRIJWILLIGER**
Wat hebben we niet vaak gezegd en ons zelf heilig beloofd ... Zoo gauw we straks maar even de kans krijgen zullen we eens laten zien wat wij Hollanders kunnen....
Vraagt daarom de nieuwe brochure met volledige inlichtingen over het instituut der oorlogsvrijwilligers bij het      —
**BUREAU A. O. V.,          HEUVEL 75A**
Reserve kapitein D. Schipper Hoofd A.O.V.
D O E T    D I T    N O G    H E D E N ! !

An appeal for volunteers shortly after liberation (early Nov 1944) in the Dutch newspaper, *Het Nieuwsblad van het Zuiden.*

Emblem of Dutch Fleet Air Arm.

# CHAPTER 10
# VICTORIOUS!

*'Let us pray that peace be now restored to the world and that God will preserve it always.'*
General Douglas MacArthur on accepting the Japanese surrender [1]

In May 1945, the war against Germany came to an end. 'Victory in Europe Day', otherwise VE Day, saw a great explosion of excitement and celebrations and the event is generally remembered by those who witnessed it. Millions were caught up in the celebrations, singing and dancing into the night. Street parties were hurriedly organised, utilising borrowed trestle tables erected in the carriageways. Despite rationing, a concerted effort was made to provide the finest possible spread, with special treats for the children. Bunting was strung between properties, Union Jacks hung from bedroom windows and the streets became a blaze of colour. Residents danced to the 'hokey cokey', the conga, and other popular dances accompanied by a piano, or gramophone, which had been hurriedly transported from front rooms into the streets for the occasion. In Stafford, the Mayor (Councillor Wallace Copeland) toured the streets[2], and at Trentham Gardens a huge victory bonfire was lit, the logs for the blaze having been collected by German prisoners of war.[3] Canadian John Anderson, then in training at HMS Fledgling,can distinctly recall the excitement of the victory celebrations and 'having a fine, rowdy time in Stafford on VE Day!'[4] Likewise, fellow countryman Jim Gilchrist and his colleagues celebrated *'in fine style'* in Eccleshall. However, on the evening of VE Day, celebrations sadly turned to fighting at the Duke of York public house, Mill Meece. The main opponents were Canadians from HMS Fledgling and locally based US. troops. Apparently, the fighting resulted from *'a debate as to who had contributed most to win the war!'* In desperation, the publican telephoned the naval base for assistance and, eventually, peace was restored.[5]

Courtesy of Mrs M Kennedy

Wrens from HMS Fledgling with naval ratings from Hednesford, taken after
a 'Wings for Victory' parade in Stafford, 13th May 1943.

Even so, for some the war was far from over. There remained the continued deadly conflict in the Far East, with millions of allied troops still engaged in fighting the Japanese. Consequently, whilst there was a sense of elation that hostilities in Europe had come to an end, the war against Japan was then to gain momentum. Thousands of tons of bombs were dropped on Tokyo by American bombers, subsequently eclipsed by the nuclear bombing of Hiroshima and Nagasaki. Finally, Japan capitulated and on 15th August Emperor Hirohito broadcast to his people that the war was over. General Douglas MacArthur accepted the Japanese surrender on 2nd September on the battleship USS Missouri in Tokyo Bay, and on 12th September in Singapore, Admiral Lord Louis Mountbatten accepted the unconditional surrender of the Japanese forces in South East Asia.

'Victory over Japan Day' (or VJ Day) on 15th August 1945, saw another upsurge of joy and celebrations. The local media reported that, whereas the streets of Stafford were *'not as gaily decorated'* as for VE Day, *'nevertheless crowds turned out in spite of drenching rain throughout the day.'* The Guildhall was decorated with the flags of the allied nations, and several shops in the town centre exhibited special window displays. The bells of the Parish Church of St. Mary rang out at intervals throughout the day, and at night the building was floodlit. Street parties were much in evidence, and a beacon was lit on Kingston Hill. In addition, celebratory dances were held in Stafford's Borough Hall, the British Restaurant, and at the English Electric Factory.[6]

In the meantime at HMS Fledgling, Second Officer Wren Audrey Deacon recorded in her diary that there had been *'rumours, and denials of rumours'* for days that Japan had surrendered. Every radio news bulletin was being listened to and on the evening of 14th August, they were inclined to believe that there was going to be no surrender. However, they had not long retired to bed when there were *'shouts and whistlings'* outside! The Wren Officer looked out of the door of her quarters to ascertain what was happening, and *'was greeted by a dustbin lid rolling along the corridor!'* Apparently, the surrender had been formally announced at midnight by Prime Minister Clement Attlee. Everyone rose and went outside, and the ship's bell was rung with such gusto that the duty fire party, manned by a Dutch crew, turned out looking for evidence of flames and smoke! As it happened, a bonfire had been prepared in anticipation of the surrender announcement, crowned with an effigy of Emperor Hirohito. This was duly lit, making *'a wonderful blaze.'* At the same time, the wardroom piano was carried outside onto the grass, and English and Dutch songs were sung to its accompaniment. There was dancing around the bonfire and a barrel of beer was 'broached', before everyone eventually retired to their quarters at around 3.30am. Fortunately for all concerned, the Captain ordered that the day *'should follow Sunday routine'*. Consequently, after a special Thanksgiving for Victory Service, many of the crew returned to their beds! However, in the evening, the celebrations continued with a show *'of an Anglo-Dutch variety'* and a ship's dance. Mrs Deacon's diary also records that she spliced the main brace that evening - her first taste, which she *'didn't like very much!'* Strictly speaking, Wrens were not entitled to participate in the naval tradition, but as she rightly observed - *'one doesn't win a war every day!'*[7]

At the same time, celebrations were, of course, taking place at neighbouring 'parent' establishment HMS Daedalus II, in Newcastle-under-Lyme, with members of the crew visiting local hostelries and joining in the spontaneous dancing in the streets. Members of the ship's crew and local residents were reputedly joining in the popular 'hokey cokey' and conga dances until well into the early hours. Here, however, events were also marked with a Victory Parade. According to the local press, the parade was one of the largest seen in the town, attended by huge crowds despite the rain. In reporting the occasion, special mention is also made of the attendance of the Royal Navy band and contingent who *'made a smart turn out'* After the parade, all those participating joined the Mayor and Mayoress (Alderman & Mrs F.T. Brant) in St.Giles Parish Church for a service of thanksgiving. The church was filled to capacity, and the service was relayed by tannoy to the crowds outside in Red Lion Square.[8]

Surprisingly, perhaps, there are those who have no doubt that the festivities and celebrations took place, but have no recollection of them. Some simply recall a feeling of disbelief that hostilities had ceased, followed by an immense sense of relief. They were certainly not alone in this respect.

World War II was the worst war of all. According to historians Edward Davidson and Dale Manning the conflict affected more than 200 nations and brought misery and death to millions.[9] The death toll figures vary according to the reference books consulted, but Sir Martin Gilbert puts the number at 50 million. This includes soldiers of all nations involved, together with civilian casualties.[10] Even so, official figures will never tell the true story of the bravery, pain and loss, or the devastating effect on families and relationships. There were also those who, having lost loved ones, or had them seriously wounded, were left wondering whether the cost was really worth the price.

*'If man would only serve for peace,*
*As he has served for war,*
*What a heaven this world would be,*
*A land worth working for.'* [11]

## NOTES

1  Quoted by Edward Davidson & Dale Manning in Chronology of World War II (Cassell)
2  Staffordshire Advertiser 19 May 1945
3  Sentinel. 8th May 1945
4  John Anderson. op.cit
5  Joan Cole. Telephone interview with author 29 January 2002
6  Staffordshire Advertiser  18 August & 8 September 1945
7  Mrs A.D. Deacon. op.cit.  p174
8  Sentinel 14 May 1945
9  Edward Davidson & Dale Manning. op.cit  p255
10  Sir Martin Gilbert. The Day The War Ended. (Harper Collins) p101
11  Extract from poem by Stanley Smart, quoted in Staffordshire Advertiser 6 January 1945

American service personnel at Yarnfield during prayers on V.E. Day.

# CHAPTER 11

# EPILOGUE

*'HMS Fledgling was a happy, lively establishment, and much of the credit for this was due to the CO.'*

Former Supt.Wren Joan Cole CBE[1]

HMS Fledgling was 'paid off' (ie decommissioned) on 31 January 1946, by which time many of the ship's company had already been drafted to other establishments or left the service.[2] It was, according to former L/Wren Dorothy Oates *'a time of great sadness to us all, our friends were leaving one after the other.'*[3] In addition, the last of the qualified Dutch trainees had left to serve with Fleet Air Arm squadrons in various parts of Britain. Those not having completed their training, together with remaining Dutch interpreters and instructors, were drafted to RAF Langham, Norfolk, which had been offered on a temporary basis by the RAF as a training centre. In fact, Langham was to prove an important training establishment for the Netherlands, as both its Royal Air Force and Fleet Air Arm personnel were trained there before the country was once more fully capable of providing its own facilities. According to Gerard Mutsaars *'the energy and perseverance of staff and trainees were the reasons that Langham was so successful.'* In 1997, to commemorate their 50th anniversary, veterans of the Royal Netherlands Air Force revisited Langham and presented a plaque inscribed with the badges of the RAF and Dutch Fleet Air Arm and bearing the words *'thank you for all you have done for us.'*[4]

One of the last items of correspondence to be written from HMS Fledgling was that to Mr J. Bennison at nearby Mill Meece Farm. In this the writer expresses gratitude for the kindness shown by the Bennison family during the period of the ship's commission. Reference is not only made to the loan of a piano for the mess, and use of the family's tennis court, but also *'the many occasions'* on which officers and ratings were entertained at the home. The letter is surviving evidence of the excellent relationship which was built up between the naval establishment and the local community.[5]

Reference is often made locally to the term 'Yarnfield Docks', some contending that the expression has associations with the former naval establishment and/or originates from that period. As one might perhaps expect, public opinion seems to differ on the matter, and evidence appears to be lacking to support the contentions. It is certainly not the only term with maritime connections in North Staffordshire. In nearby Newcastle-under-Lyme, former home of HMS Daedalus II, one frequently hears reference to 'Knutton Banana Docks'. The origins of this also appear to be lost in time, but it nevertheless has been the subject of many entertaining debates in local hostelries and will, no doubt, continue to be so. There is certainly no shortage of theories as to the origin, nor people to suggest them, but

Old accommodation blocks, HMS Fledgling, through MOD fencing, Old Hall Lane.

Remains of HMS Fledgling's firing butts on private land off Old Hall Lane.

Former HMS Fledgling hangar, now in agricultural use, on private land off Old Hall Lane.
These photographs all taken by the author in 1997.

again evidence is lacking. However, in relation to 'Yarnfield Docks' a number of people have suggested that the expression may originate from a time when sluice gates were placed on a stream near to the village green. Whilst these were supposedly installed to prevent flooding, an expanse of water was created which some residents are said to have threatened to put boats on! I leave readers to draw their own conclusions.

Following the decommissioning of HMS Fledgling, the site remained in the hands of the Admiralty, it being recommissioned as HMS Caballa. References to this may be found in the local authority records, the establishment existing from 1946-48.[6] Designated as an Education Voluntary Training (EVT) unit, HMS Caballa fulfilled a valuable role in providing training facilities for personnel who were about to leave the service and re-enter civvy street. Subsequently, the site was used variously as No.4 Police Training College, and then by Messrs Laings for residential and administrative purposes during the period of the company's contract for construction of the M6 motorway. In addition, the hangars were used as an overflow storage facility by the Royal Navy Transport Depot at Clayton (formerly part of the site of HMS Daedalus II).

From time to time, former Fledgling personnel have returned to the area, attempting to rediscover old haunts and to revisit the location of their old base. Such ventures have not always proved successful. Some have had difficulty in actually identifying the site and, of course, only certain long term residents would be able to provide directions, if requested to do so. Even enquiries at police stations have not always been fruitful!

The problem is perhaps compounded because the greater part of the former Fledgling site, and that of the former Royal Ordnance Factory, remain in the hands of the Ministry of Defence. Surrounded by high security fencing, this vast area continues to be used for military purposes. Not surprisingly, this is strongly resented in some quarters! I understand that it is possible to obtain permission to gain access to the Fledgling site at times, but otherwise glimpses of the former accommodation blocks, etc, may be seen from certain points outside the fencing. Also remains of the establishment's firing butts exist on private land off Old Hall Lane, together with three hangars now in use for agricultural purposes. These are not readily evident and, as one former Wren commented, having attempted to find trace of the camp - 'it's as if Fledgling never existed!'[7]

NOTES

1   Joan Cole. Telephone interview with author 29 January 2002
2   Lt.Cdr B. Warlow RN. *Shore Establishments of the Royal Navy* (Maritime Books) p 56
3   Dorothy Oates. op.cit
4   Ex information Gerard Mutsaars.
5   Lt.Cdr(E) W.E. Budge to Mr J.Bennison 23 January 1946
6   Stone RDC. *Minutes of Eccleshall & Chebsey Sewerage & Water Supply Committee* Dec 1947
7   Dorothy M. Brewer. Letter to author 25 September 1997

Lynne Bebbington

The author with former Dutch naval officer,
Gerard Mutsaars, in Antwerp June 2002.

# BIBLIOGRAPHY

In addition to those works quoted in the source notes, I found the following useful:

*The Squadrons of the Fleet Air Arm* by Ray Sturtivant & Theo Ballance (Air-Britain)

*Britannia's Daughters* by Ursula Stuart Mason (Leo Cooper)

*The Story of the WRNS* by Eileen Bigland (Nicholson & Watson)

*Blue for a Girl* by John A. Drummond (W. H. Allen)

*Women Who Went to War* by Eric Taylor (Grafton Books)